Granite Ware

Collectors' Guide with Prices

Book II

Vernagene Vogelzang and Evelyn Welch

Photography (unless otherwise credited): Vernagene Vogelzang

Cover design, interior layout: Ann Eastburn

On the front cover: Marcia Breon's kitchen display includes Cottolene enameled pie pan, a gray spoon, measuring cup, and a biscuit cutter.

Library of Congress Catalog
Card Number 80-51583

ISBN 0-87069-458-8

10 9 8 7 6 5 4 3

Published by

Wallace-Homestead Book Company
201 King of Prussia Road
Radnor, Pennsylvania 19089

One of the ABC PUBLISHING Companies

Contents

Preface and Acknowledgments

This book was written to elaborate on facts from our first book, and to increase the general knowledge and appreciaticn of the lively and spirited granite ware industry, which lasted more than seventy years in the United States.

We were encouraged by the enthusiastic response to our first book and were grateful for suggestions from collectors and reviewers. All the material in this book is new, with the exception of information we needed to repeat to make this a clear and complete work. We even have a new spelling for granite ware because "Graniteware®" has become a registered trademark.

In preparing this book, we were fortunate in contacting two men who spent their lives working in the enameling industry. Woodrow Carpenter, chairman of the board of the Ceramic Coating Company, Newport, Kentucky, introduced us to Merlin H. Whitehead, a classmate of Carpenter's at the University of Illinois, who worked for some of the largest granite ware manufacturers.

Both men are expert consultants, providing technical information and photographs. We thank them, plus three other people who gave us special assistance: Dr. Doris Beuttenmuller, Webster University, St. Louis, Missouri; Mrs. Bernice Morehouse, The Meriden Historical Society, Meriden, Connecticut; and Mr. J. Daniel Hines, Granite City Steel, Granite City, Illinois.

We also are thankful for the invaluable help of the following:

The collectors and consultants: Jo Allers, Bonnie and Chuck Badger, Marcia and Del Breon, Tommy Bruhn, Mary Jane and Jean Joseph Castagne, Betty Cole, Marianne Comiskey, Reginald P. Corrigeux, Jo Ann Costley, Jo An A. Dentler, Elaine and Larry Erwin, Mr. and Mrs. John Freter, Sybil Garibaldi, Colleen Gradowski, Sharlene and Russell A. Harrison, Brenda Hutto, Beverly Johnson, Bruce Johnson, Evelyn Jolliff, Marnette Kilburn, Louise M. Loehr, Fredrick A. Petersen, Jean Phillips, Jay and Joan Smith, Von Ceil Smith, Nancy Splitstoser, and Phyllis and Randy Tomkins.

The photographers: Chuck Badger, Marianne Comiskey, Bill Farmer, John Freter, Ray Moore, Jay Smith, and Fred Splitstoser.

Introduction

Tourists in Venice line up and file into St. Mark's Cathedral to see the Pala d'Oro, a great Byzantine reredos with more than eighty enameled panels set against a gold screen adorned with large, uncut precious stones. There are three hundred emeralds, three hundred sapphires, ninety rubies, four hundred garnets, ninety amethysts, four topazes, two antique cameos, and thirteen hundred pearls. The panels, it is believed, were confiscated by the Venetians from a monastery in Constantinople in the thirteenth century. The finely wrought enamels are treasured more than the jewels.

Enameling has been an art form since its development in ancient China and Egypt. It has continued as such to the present. In the 1940's, Benito Quinquela Martin created large-scale, enameled murals. This talented Argentinean artist's portrayals of laborers at work and Buenos Aires port scenes are alive with movement and power. Today, Norio Hara is Japan's brilliant master of cloisonné.

In the 1850s, however, enameling veered another direction — from art to commerce. And it was granite ware that made the transition. The mass production of enameled cookware, a comparatively recent phenomenon, was the first commercial use of enameling on metals and the most important industrial use of enameling.

In order to transcend the endeavors of art, manufacturers adapted enameling for commerce. Certainly it was not possible to coat pans by the same methods used to enamel translucent windows in European cathedrals.

Chemists, metallurgists, and engineers were needed. Two chemists, Andrew Irving Andrews of the University of Illinois and Maynard King of Ohio State University, were the forerunners in this field. They were instrumental in developing departments of ceramic engineering at their universities.

In the early 1930s, the Enameled Utensils Manufacturers' Council was formed under the direction of Fredrick A. Petersen. The council conducted a research program in the Department of Ceramic Engineering at the University of Illinois to develop improved enamels and to study the effects of the design of products on properties, such as impact and thermal shock. The council also conducted forums at which the technical representatives of all member companies could discuss material and production problems.

Petersen, a professor at Ohio State University, said, "In the days of 'Agate Ware' and 'Mottled Gray Ware,' the enameler was the key man, since he controlled the formulations which, in many cases, had been handed down to him from prior generations. He had the secret additives to reduce or eliminate defects that might be encountered due to certain conditions, such as frit milling, enamel application, drying, or firing."

One such enameler was H. D. Carter of the Canton Stamping and Enameling Company. "As for frit formulations and the mechanical aspects of the application of porcelain enamels, Carter had no equal in the whole world," said Merlin Whitehead, a co-worker of Carter's who has worked for some of the largest granite ware manufacturers.

Eventually, a quarterly trade journal, *The Enamelist*, was published. It contributed to the promotion of ceramic and surface-coating technology, and it included articles on product control, plant supervision, and a variety of applicable research.

The progress of the porcelain enamel industry from 1930 to 1950 was a landmark of free enterprise in the United States, according to Harold P. Connare in *The Enamelist*. Its achievements propelled the industry to the stature of big business and made it a significant force that contributed to new and improved standards of living.

Throughout enameling's history, then, the transition from art to commerce has been accomplished, and the two avenues have become equally valuable.

Early Experiments and Patents

In the enameling industry, there were many charitable and creative inventors who recorded their experiments for the benefit of those who followed. Jacob J. Vollrath was one. His December 6, 1881, patent for marbleizing granite ware declares, "The following to be a full, clear, and exact description of the invention such as will enable others skilled in the art to which it appertains to make and use the same, reference being had to the accompanying drawings, and to letters or figures of reference marked thereon."

The earliest account for "Enameling of Vessels For The Kitchen" was found in the 1803 *Encyclopedia Britannica*. In 1779, the Society of Emulation in Paris offered a prize for the discovery of a composition that would be better than copper, lead, tin, or glazed earthenware in making kitchen utensils. The Society wanted something that was strong, inexpensive, and capable of bearing the highest heat of kitchen fire and the most sudden changes from heat to cold.

In the same year, Sven Rinman of the Royal Academy of Stockholm was experimenting with enameling copper and hammered iron vessels, and he submitted his work to the Society. Although the encyclopedia does not state whether or not Rinman won the prize, he certainly deserved it, for he performed thirteen experiments. Some were successful and others failed.

Nine were on copper and four involved hammered iron. Rinman noted that cast iron was too thick to be heated quickly, and quick heating was necessary to prevent scaling of the enamel.

In an experiment on copper, he made a paste of powdered glass and water and brushed it on. After the vessel had dried, it was heated gradually and then exposed to sudden and violent heat, partly in a coal fire fanned by a pair of bellows and partly in an assaying furnace.

The mixture melted into an opaque white enamel that covered the surface of the copper evenly and was bonded firmly to the metal. The enamel was acid resistant, did not break easily, and liquids could be boiled in it. The problem with this procedure was that it required greater heat than was commonly obtained in an assaying furnace.

In his next experiments, Rinman added substances to make the mixture more fusible.

All of Rinman's efforts were directed toward solving the problems of heating, acid resistance, economy, color and luster, and adherance to metal — identical and persistent concerns of the kitchenware industry. Rinman concluded that his experiments on enameling iron kitchen utensils might prove useful for other purposes, such as preserving iron from rust and calcination.

Following the lengthy account of Rinman's work *The English Cyclopaedia* included a brief reference to a patent obtained by a Dr. Hickling in 1799 for two methods of enameling kitchen utensils. Enameled wares were manufactured under this patent for some time until the patent was given up. There was no more information about the patent, where it was registered, or even Dr. Hickling's full name.

The various processes in the practice of enameling, like the composition of enamels, have probably never been completely made known to the public; they require extraordinary care and attention, and artists who may have been so fortunate as to discover any improved mode of operating are commonly too jealous to make it known.

The English Cyclopaedia, 1867

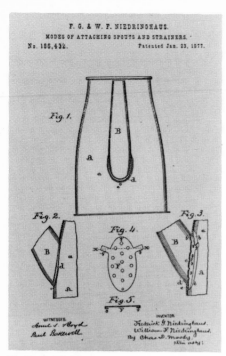

F. G. & W. F. Niedringhaus, "Modes of Attaching Spouts and Strainers, Patented Jan. 23, 1877."

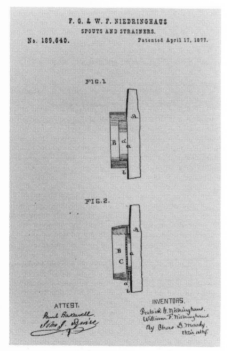

F. G. & W. F. Niedringhaus, "Spouts and Strainers, Patented April 17, 1877."

In 1839, Thomas and Charles Clarke applied for an enameling patent. This patent was of particular importance because it mentioned clay as a mill addition. "This is the first mention of clay as a mill addition that I have ever seen," noted Woodrow Carpenter. Clay has been used as a bonding agent in making enamels ever since.

The Clarke's patent specified formulas for glazes and gave methods of cleaning the vessels and applying enamels. It explained how to cool and fire the ware and included exact temperatures for firing. The patent was so detailed that, when other manufacturers began producing high-quality enameled ware, the Clarkes thought their work had been stolen, and they sued for an invasion of their patent rights. The Court of Exchequer, however, felt that the formulas by which a good enamel might be compounded were almost enumerable, and that a patent for such a purpose seemed untenable or at least easily evaded.

The earliest American patent that we have been able to find is Charles Stümer's "Improvement in Enamels for Iron," New York, July 25, 1848. Our first book includes excerpts from this patent.

Another patent, by George W. Holley for the "Improvement in Enameling Cast-Iron," Niagara, New York, was described by Woodrow Carpenter, chairman of the board of the Ceramic Coating Company, Newport, Kentucky, and "concerned pouring molten metal into a casting mold lined with enamel. When the mold was removed, the cast iron part was coated with enamel. I have known two people who tried it during the past fifty years, but it never worked."

Holley described a novel way to separate the casting from the mold in his patent of March 10, 1857. This procedure used sour flour or molasses mixed with sand to cover the side of the core plate that was to be coated. When this was baked until the surface of the sand was hardened, the enamel was spread over the hardened sand. The enamel then was fired. The melted iron was poured into the mold, with the intention of melting or softening the enamel so that it would adhere to the iron as it became cold. At the same time, the sand and molasses mixture would have softened enough to allow the easy removal of the casting from the mold.

Another patent, indicating the diversity of the experiments, was by George A. Burrough of Providence, Rhode Island. Dated May 30, 1871, the patent was for coating metal articles, such as pipes and fittings, couplings, elbows, submerged pumps, letters for signs, and the cardinal numbers or figures for numbering houses or streets.

In our research, we have studied patents for three large manufacturers: the Niedringhaus Brothers, Vollrath, and Lalance and Grosjean. These patents describe how granite ware was made, and how it was enameled and decorated. They also reveal the character of the inventor, providing a sense of who the man was, his enthusiasm for his work, and his determination to find out how to solve a problem. The problems ranged from making a better hinge on a coffeepot lid to attaching a handle with a rivet in the vertical seam to eliminate the need for an extra rivet. On the following pages, you will find excerpts from several of these patents to give you a feeling for the extraordinary inventors and their work.

We know that the St. Louis Stamping Company made granite ware in 1874, because we have a cookbook dated June 9, 1874. However, the first patent found for Frederick G. and William F. Niedringhaus is dated May 30, 1876. The patent concerns the improvement of enameling sheet-iron ware by means of selective etching.

The metal is cleaned, in the usual way, in an acid-bath; then without employing an alkali-bath, it is, after the usual scouring to remove the scale, placed in clear water, and allowed to remain, say, at least half an hour, and so as to remove the acid. As soon as it is taken from the water, it is immediately coated with a liquid glaze and placed in the drying-room, where the glaze is slowly dried thereon. The appearance and character of the enamel are determined during this drying of the glaze, as according to the length of the time taken in the drying, and to the temperature of the drying-room, will be the amount of oxidation. No definite rule can be given for either, as the process is affected by many circumstances — as, for instance, the humidity of the atmosphere.

We prepare our glaze from the ordinary ingredients, taking care to have the ingredients mixed and thoroughly smelted together in bulk, to expel all carbon and other elements that would impede oxidation, and in order that the acid in the glaze may have free action. They are then ground in water, and applied in the usual way.

Now, by reason of the presence of the acid of the glaze, an oxidation of the metallic base takes place freely during the drying process, and appearing in and throughout the glaze as reddish spots. This causes the enamel, when it is finally formed, in the usual way, by baking the ware in the oven, to assume the desired mottled appearance. By reason of this oxidation, also, the enamel is caused to enter the pores of the iron, and become more intimately incorporated with the metal, thus rendering the enamel more durable.

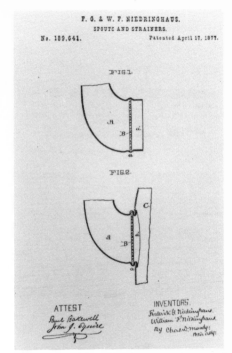

F. G. & W. F. Niedringhaus, "Spouts and Strainers, Patented April 17, 1877."

Another way to accomplish the same results when retaining the alkali-bath, the patent continued, was to increase the boracic acid and lessen the alkaline fluxes in the glaze, overcoming the alkali and oxidizing the metal. The amount of acid in the glaze affected the character of the mottling, but the process did not prevent the addition of the usual coloring matter to the glaze.

William F. Niedringhaus' patent, dated July 31, 1877, concerned cooling the enameled ware slowly after it was taken from the baking oven. Customarily, it had been allowed to cool freely in the open air, but Niedringhaus believed that was detrimental. He wrote:

To fuse the enamel upon the iron base, the ware must, as is well understood, be carried to a high degree of heat, In cooling down from this high temperature the iron base naturally contracts in a much longer ratio than the now-formed enamel-coating, especially when the latter is essentially a glass, the kind I preferably employ. Now, if the cooling operation is allowed to proceed rapidly the iron chills and shrinks before the enamel has become properly incorporated in and attached to it, and in consequence the enamel is not reliably adhesive, but, in use, splinters off.

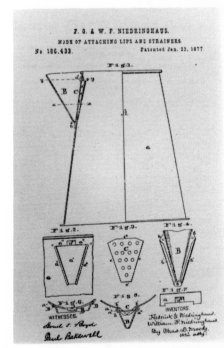

F. G. & W. F. Niedringhaus, "Modes of Attaching Lips and Strainers, Patented Jan. 23, 1877."

To solve this problem, Niedringhaus suggested prolonging the cooling of the ware as long as practicable. As soon as the ware could be taken from the baking oven and handled without injuring the enamel, it was placed in an environment in which the temperature was the same as the ware. It was cooled slowly in a four-to-six-hour period. This rendered the enamel more malleable, but the process was particularly valuable in that it strengthened the union between the iron and the enamel.

The following Niedringhaus patents were for improved ways of assembling enamelware. Photographs of the artists' drawings are shown in this section.

A patent dated January 23, 1877, concerned attaching spouts and strainers. Customarily, spouts were either soldered to the body of the vessel or fastened by means of a double-lock seam. Neither of these methods was satisfactory. Solder melted easily, the double-lock seam was difficult and expensive to form, and the seam did not heat and cool evenly.

The patent proposed to overcome these difficulties by projecting the spout through the side of the vessel and turning the inside flange up against the body and around the opening. The strainer was secured in position by lugs that were folded under the flange of the spout. A rivet fastened these parts together at the lower end of the opening.

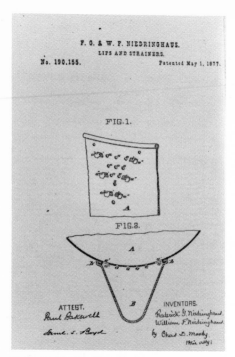

F. G. & W. F. Niedringhaus, "Lips and Strainers, Patented May 1, 1877."

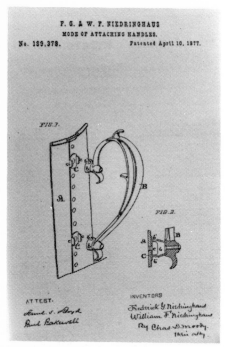

F. G. & W. F. Niedringhaus, "Mode of Attaching Handles, Patented April 10, 1877."

A second patent for the improvement of attaching spouts and strainers was dated April 17, 1877. It concerned attaching a metallic spout to an enameled body by means of soldering. The patented process explained how a collar made of a metal to which enamel would not readily adhere was fitted into a vessel. A strainer was fastened into the collar when the outside of the collar was slightly contracted. When the vessel, collar, and strainer were enameled, the enamel on the collar easily splintered off. Then the spout could be soldered to the collar. This was patent number 189,640, shown in this section.

A third patent for applying spouts and strainers, dated April 17, 1877, specified that the "spout is made ready for attachment by swelling it slightly outward so as to form a fold." The strainer was then sprung into the fold, and the inner end of the spout was passed into the body as far as the fold. Then the end was turned up on the inside of the body, forming a flange around the spout opening. The fold on the outside of the body was flattened, and the enameling closed the joint and gave the vessel a finished appearance.

A patent dated January 23, 1877, described a method of attaching lips and strainers to vessels by means other than the customary soldering. When vessels such as coffee boilers or milk buckets were heated to the high temperature needed for enameling, the solder melted and did not hold the lips in place.

In this patent, F. G. and W. F. Niedringhaus recommended locking the lips and strainers firmly together by means of flanges and rivets, then further strengthening the joints by enameling. They noted that this was not only a better way to secure the lips and strainers, but also was economical.

Their patent, dated May 1, 1877, proposed another improvement in lips and strainers, wherein the upper part of a vessel was perforated to form the strainer and to receive the lip.

The strainer was formed by a series of perforations in which the metal was entirely removed. The lip was fastened in place by closing the flanges, made by another set of perforations from which the metal was only partly cut away. Three rivets were inserted at the corners of the base of the lip, and the joint was strengthened by the enamel covering.

The Niedringhauses wrote that the strainer could be formed and the lip attached in an inexpensive manner. The construction was durable, and the appearance was neat.

A patent dated April 10, 1877, related a method of attaching handles to vessels by soldering. Metal ears were riveted to an enameled vessel, then soldered to the metal sockets on a handle. The handle could be made of any material, but the ears and the sockets had to be of tin, brass, or a substance to which the solder would adhere.

"Improvement in Sheet-Metal Vessel-Handles," dated July 3, 1877, related that a long rivet would be passed from the inside of the vessel outward through the wall then through and beyond the handle. The handle could then be fastened in position by applying solder to form a head. This was significant because, as the patent explained:

> By means of this projecting rivet it is evident a vessel-body can be readily prepared to be sold as an article of merchandise, to which any suitable handle can be subsequently attached by the purchaser without injury to the enamel, thus adapting it to the present requirements of the trade.

Manning-Bowman may have purchased ware and attached the company's own ornate White Metal Mountings. A patent dated April 17, 1877, for the "Improvement in Hinges of Vessels of Enameled Iron-ware," stated the aim to provide a neat, inexpensive, and durable hinge.

The strap of the hinge was folded at its center around a wire that usually encircled the top of the vessel, and its ends were then passed through a slot in the cover, opened apart, and turned down on the upper side of the cover. Solder was applied to and between the ends to form a head on the strap and to prevent its being withdrawn through the slot. The metal of the strap was a type to which solder adhered.

The last of the Niedringhaus' patents that we have seen was dated May 1, 1877. It concerned the "Improvement in Joints of Vessels of Enameled Sheet-Iron Ware."

This patent stated that the bottom of the vessel should be provided with a downwardly projecting flange that would come against the lower end of the side when the bottom was in place. These parts then were turned outward, up, and over to form a double hollow bead that locked the side and bottom of the vessel together. When the enamel coating was applied, it caulked the joint and gave a finish to the construction.

Jacob J. Vollrath's patent, dated December 6, 1881, concerned:

> Improvements in the art or process of enameling iron, and iron and metal articles in general, whereby the enamel coating is made to adhere firmly to the iron and has a beautifully marbleized or variegated surface of any desired color or design.

Vollrath prepared the surface of the metal articles through the ordinary pickling, scouring, and washing operations. He noted that the art of enameling metals, as commonly conducted, called for several coats of enamel: a body coat to unite the iron with itself; a second coat, usually colored with some metallic oxide to ornament the article; and often a third coat to impart a glaze or polish.

Vollrath stated that the success and superiority of his process depended on the nature of the compositions employed and in the way the surface coating was applied.

> In all known processes the marbled, mottled, or spotted appearance of the enameled surface is caused by the oxidation of the metal surface during the operation of drying the enameling composition thereon.
>
> It has been proposed to make the glaze or enamel ornamental by tinting or coloring the same with any suitable coloring matter, but no process heretofore known involves the production of a marbleized surface in a systematic manner without depending on the oxidation of the metal for attaining the desired result.

Materials listed were melted together and spread on the surface of the article by dipping or pouring. The body coating was allowed to dry so that it would not crack or craze during the first firing. A second coating — a porcelain preparation — was applied, and the ware was fired again.

> A final coating or a composition for producing the marbleized or variegated surface is then applied to the second coating, and is the same as the latter, with the addition of the desired coloring matter. For producing a blue color, potter's blue is added, and for a red color fifteen per cent of oxide of iron and two per cent of manganese are used in the marbleizing composition. The latter is spread on the surface to be ornamented, and is run over the same by properly manipulating the article, so as to cause the composition to form the desired veins, streaks, or other designs.
>
> A suitable stencil or an impression block or form may be used for applying the marbleized composition in a more systematic manner than when applied by hand-manipulation alone.
>
> When white marble is to be imitated the ground is white, with gray spots, and for giving the appearance of red marble a copper-colored red coating, with white spots, is used, and for blue marble blue spots are added.
>
> The marbleizing composition is applied to the vitrified or porcelain surface caused by burning on the second coating, as is firmly affixed thereon by subjecting it to the same temperature as said porcelain surface..

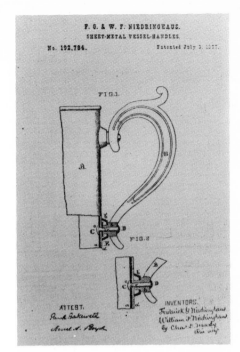

F. G. & W. F. Niedringhaus, "Sheet-Metal Vessel-Handles Patented July 3, 1877."

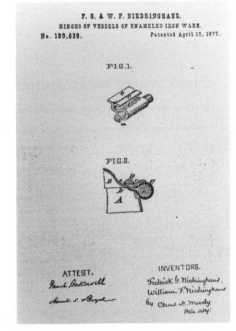

F. G. & W. F. Niedringhaus, "Hinges of Vessels of Enameled Iron Ware, Patented April 17, 1877."

11

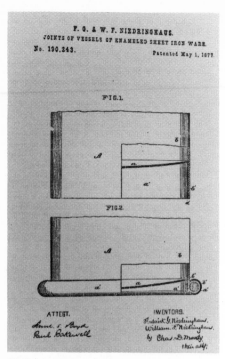

F. G. & W. F. Niedringhaus, "Joints of Vessels of Enameled Sheet Iron Ware, Patented May 1, 1877."

Carl A. W. Vollrath, assignor to the Jacob J. Vollrath Manufacturing Company of Sheboygan, Wisconsin, invented a new "'Process of Enameling Metal Surfaces," dated November 19, 1889.

After ordinary pickling or scouring operations, he prepared a ground coat, applied it to an article, and fired it. His finishing coat was made of two mixtures — "A" and "B". Both consisted of enameling ingredients that were melted, cooled, and ground together. However, color was added to Mixture "B," and it was ground to a different degree of fineness than Mixture "A". The two were mixed together to a pastelike consistency, then were applied by pouring or dipping. When the ware was fired, the coarse particles melted at a slower rate and formed the mottled pattern.

These early experiments and patents indicate that many creative minds and energized spirits contributed to the development of enameled kitchenwares. Beginning with Sven Rinman in 1779, and continuing with Dr. Hickling, the Clarkes, Stümer, Holley, Burrough, the Niedringhauses, and the Vollraths, the production of this fine cookware became an actuality through the steady efforts of many industrious innovators.

Granite Ware Manufacturers, Jobbers, and Retailers

The pioneers, the men and women who came to the United States from all over the world, brought with them a curiosity, energy, intelligence, and motivation. Some of them became involved in the manufacturing of granite ware. They were smelters, draw-press operators, engineers who designed special equipment, sorters and wrappers, and salesmen. In recognition of these pioneers, we are presenting the history of one company, which is representative of the many manufacturing companies that participated in the Industrial Revolution.

History of the St. Louis Stamping Company

Frederick Niedringhaus came to the United States in 1855, at the age of eighteen. He had learned glazing, painting, and the tinner's trade in his father's shop in Luebbecke, Westphalia, Germany. When he arrived in St. Louis, he began working at the tinner's bench. He was paid four dollars each week, and out of this he saved one dollar and a half.

Six months later, his brother, William, joined him. Later, his parents, Frederick and Marie, and several other brothers also emigrated to the United States.

Frederick and William worked together as apprentice tinners and roofers for two years, until they saved enough money to start their own tin shop. A story, passed down through the trade, tells how the two sold their wares.

In the early days, working on opposite sides of the street, each brother walked, carrying big wicker baskets full of tinware on his shoulders. One would call out, "Pots and pans and kitchen kettles," while the other, whose English was more limited, cried, "Me too! Me too!"

The Niedringhauses' business was successful from the beginning. The next step was stamping tinware, beginning in 1862.

The following quotations are from *The Granite City Steel Company; History of an American Enterprise*, by Doris Beuttenmuller.

> America's material greatness can be traced directly to its feat of pioneering the modern miracle of mass production and its indispensable corollary, mass distribution.
> — Earl Lifshey, *The Housewares Story*, 1973

During those early years, tinware was cut by hand and soldered together. However, in that age of rapidly developing machinery, improved methods were soon discovered. Tinware manufacturers in France developed a machine which stamped out pots and pans from a single sheet of tin plate. This machine produced shiny, lightweight kitchen utensils far superior to the castiron vessels then in use, and much more attractive. As soon as possible, the brothers imported one of the machines and a workman to operate it.

The St. Louis Stamping Company

In 1866, William F. and Frederick G. Niedringhaus incorporated the St. Louis Stamping Company. With small presses, they began the manufacture of kitchen utensils and in this way joined those early pioneers who helped to satisfy the demands of the American people for something finer than the previous generation had possessed.

Scanty information exists about these early years. We know that these small capitalists were both capitalists and laborers. Typical of a period in industrial history when ownership was synonymous with active management and work, the brothers labored at the machines, experimented with unfamiliar problems, and guided the efforts of their few employees.

Undoubtedly this venture required great courage. The brothers were young, with limited funds and business experience. At the same time, economic and social changes of great magnitude were in progress throughout the country. This was a period of revolution in industry as a result of science, practical innovations, and enlarged opportunities. The population was surging westward due to the growing flood of immigrants. The west was growing, towns were developing into cities, small firms into large corporations, workers into specialists. Such rapid expansion, feverish activity, ceaseless change, alarming complexity in every walk of life may have frightened some men, but to the Niedringhaus brothers, men of courage and enterprise, the enlargement of economic life meant opportunity. By hard work, spirited energy, and determination, they developed a tremendous business, and, within a short time, were prosperous manufacturers.

St. Louis Stamping Company, Second and Cass Avenue, Established in 1866
From Engraving by William Mackwitz

"St. Louis Stamping Company, Second and Cass Avenue, Established in 1866." From engraving by William Mackwitz.

Granite Ware

The brothers continued to work feverishly, spending long hours at the factory, engrossed in details of production, or absorbed in plans to capture new markets, and sometimes even taking turns at the stamping machines when rush orders piled up.

William lost his health due to overwork, and his physician advised him to forget the business, see new places, and cultivate new interests. Therefore, as soon as his health permitted, William went abroad. While traveling in Europe, he happened upon a product which he knew would promote his St. Louis business. It was in the late 1860's, when a steamboat on which he was a passenger pulled up to the wharf of a small Rhenish village to unload, that William strolled through the village and came upon a show window in which he saw displayed kitchen utensils which were coated with a glossy substance. Entering the shop, he examined the ware and found it felt as smooth as frozen satin. Realizing the potential demand for such products in the United States,

William sought the proprietor to learn how they were made. The proprietor consented to sell him the secrets of the entire process, and accordingly an agreement was quickly made. It is believed that he purchased this information for approximately $5,000.

William spent several weeks in the Rhenish factory, learning what ingredients went into the enamel and how it was applied to sheet iron. Then, armed with notes, he hurried to the nearest port and returned to St. Louis. Within a short time, he and Frederick developed and patented the process on which was founded one of the major industries of the United States — the making of "granite ware," so called because ground granite was the basic material in the enamel. Sales of the St. Louis Stamping Company doubled and redoubled as housewives sought the new utensils. As production and sales increased, the brothers became more confident and began planning the further expansion of their business.

The Granite Iron Rolling Mills

For many years, the St. Louis Stamping Company imported from Wales the sheet iron used in the manufacture of granite ware. It was the custom of the brothers to purchase an extra year's supply with each order. This proved to be an excellent policy in 1877 when the Welsh mill was destroyed by fire.

The following year, the St. Louis Stamping Company made certain of a source of supply by erecting the Granite Iron Rolling Mills at Second and Destrehan Streets in St. Louis. To obtain sheet iron which was comparable to that purchased from Wales, the company imported skilled Welsh workmen to labor in the plant.

Frederick G. Niedringhaus was president of this company and William F. was vice-president and manager.

From this humble beginning developed the Granite City Steel Company. The present company officially dates its founding as 1878, thereby recognizing the Granite Iron Rolling Mills as its earliest predecessor.

The establishment of the Granite Iron Rolling Mills enabled the St. Louis Stamping Company to stop importing sheet iron. However, it still was necessary to purchase foreign tin plate, on which the company paid a duty of $22.40 per shipping ton, because the low price of the English product had stifled the development of the tin plate industry in the United States.

In 1888, Frederick Niedringhaus was elected to the Fifty-first Congress of the United States from the Eighth Congressional District of Missouri. He was instrumental in the formulation of a tariff bill that became the McKinley Act of 1890. This was the greatest boost the United States steel industry had ever received. Within a short time, the United States became the greatest steel producer in the world, and soon the Granite Iron Rolling Mills began commercially producing tin plate. The following, from *The Granite City Steel Company*, explains the Niedringhauses' expansion.

Early Expansion

While Frederick Niedringhaus engaged in legislative activity in Washington, William devoted his time to research in the St. Louis factory. William was a keen analyst of industrial trends. Noting the revolutionary changes taking place in the economy, he anticipated the passage of the Iron Age to the Age of Steel, and realized that his company would feel the impact as the demand for iron granite ware declined. Therefore, he sought a method to enamel steel utensils. After repeated attempts and failures, he developed an enamel which expanded and contracted at the same rate as sheet steel. An open-hearth furnace was installed at the Granite Rolling Mill to manufacture steel. The uncertainty which attended initial operations was speedily dispelled, and the partners met with positive encouragement.

The business continued to flourish, and the Niedringhauses decided to expand. They made a bid on a large tract of land near the rolling mill and stamping plant, but the owners of a small but important parcel held out for an exorbitant price, and officials in St. Louis refused to vacate an unopened street, according to Nicholas P. Veeder, 1957 president of Granite City Steel.

The search for another location led across the Mississippi River and ended with the purchase of 3,500 acres of Illinois farmland about nine miles north of downtown St. Louis. Two years later, in 1894, construction of the Granite City Steel Works and the St. Louis Stamping Works was underway. The function of the steelworks was to produce steel and roll it into steel bars for the Granite Iron Rolling Mills in St. Louis.

Veeder stated that the early development of Granite City, the community that grew up around the industrial plants, was somewhat unusual for that day, because care was taken to avoid paternalism. Some members of the Niedringhaus family wanted to name their city in honor of its founders, but the brothers chose the name Granite City to commemorate the ware that was the basis of their industry. Industry laid out the town, put down sidewalks, graded and cindered the streets, provided the water supply, and even planted trees. There was a public park and free sites for churches and schools. Homes and flats were built for workmen who wanted to live there.

Property outside the plant gates was sold as quickly as possible to the residents, and the residents were responsible for local government from the start. There were 3,122 people living in Granite City in 1900 and 40,000 in 1961.

The Niedringhauses wanted to avoid the economic disadvantages of a one-industry town, and they were instrumental in attracting other companies to the area. By the early 1960s, Granite City contained a major part of the heavy industry of metropolitan St. Louis.

The new St. Louis Stamping Company plant occupied a thirty-acre site at the west end of Niedringhaus Avenue. Its principal products were granite ware and japanned, lithographed, and galvanized ware. Manufactured among the myriad kinds of pots, pans, and other containers were foot baths, coffee biggins, gold-miners' pans, and fruit jar fillers.

Frederick was president of the St. Louis Stamping Company, and William was president of Granite City Steel.

The National Enameling and Stamping Company

Frederick and William Niedringhaus reached the peak of their business careers at the end of the nineteenth century, when the three Niedringhaus plants — the St. Louis Stamping Company, the Granite Iron Rolling Mills, and the Granite City Steel Works — were consolidated with other major producers of household enameled ware, namely the Kieckhefer Plant of Milwaukee, Matthai Ingram Plant, and Keen & Haggerty Company, both of Baltimore, and the Haberman Manufacturing Company of New York.

George W. Niedringhaus, William's son, wrote in unpublished papers that the formation of the National Enameling and Stamping Company was the result of competition that had sprung up in imitation of the enameled ware made by the St. Louis Stamping Company. Suits were filed against these new firms for infringement of the patents. The resulting compromise led to the amalgamation of the companies.

The National Enameling and Stamping Company, known as NESCO, was incorporated in 1899. Frederick Niedringhaus continued as president until his retirement in 1908, after which he served as chairman of the board.

William F. Niedringhaus was the director general for the consolidation of all the plants, and George W. Niedringhaus was general manager. Dr. Beuttenmuller wrote of William F. Niedringhaus:

Although several members of the Niedringhaus family were interested in the company, it was William who emerged as a St. Louis industrialist and played the leading role in ably guiding the destinies of the company during the first fifty years as it grew from a tin shop to a manufacturer of steel and steel products. In addition to managing the company during the first years of its existence, he shaped the policies which have substantially continued in effect to this day.

William F. Niedringhaus possessed the determination and spirit of enterprise which characterized German immigrants of his time. He saw the possibilities of combining the truths of science and the skill of mechanics into new elements and producing something better than the world had had before. He introduced enamel to the United States, and developed the country's leading producer of enamelware. Other interests were organized under his leadership and carried forward to success under his management. He had the satisfaction of seeing the city he had founded grow to hold a population of 12,000 people, with churches, public schools, and a hospital. In addition to being director general of the National Enameling and Stamping Company, he was president of the

Granite City Gas, Light and Fuel Company, and one of the original promoters of the American Steel Foundry and Commonwealth Steel Company. He also was director of the Granite City National Bank, as well as the Granite City Realty Company.

Part of his success was the luck of living in a quick growing country of tremendous resources. But an equally large part was the way he went out to meet fortune. He had not only a sharp sense of opportunity but a series of particular ideas about business and business administration based upon a sense of justice, honesty, and considerate regard for his fellow man. In addition, he had the faculty of drawing to him a corps of associates whose energy and business judgment proved a valuable supplement to his own.

William died July 9, 1908. Newspaper accounts said that he died at his home in St. Louis. A committee was appointed to arrange transportation for the people of Granite City to attend the burial. All labor organizations attended, and a memorial service was held at the Niedringhaus Memorial Methodist Church.

A tribute by Florence Hayward appeared in the newspaper. It said, "His was the simplicity of real wisdom, the gentleness of true force, the full value of a life well lived from day to day."

George W., William's son, succeeded his father and was placed in complete charge of the Granite City plants. In 1919, he became president of NESCO. Under his leadership, the company expanded and its output increased.

Until 1908, the steel works had produced solely for the manufacture of household utensils. George W. found additional outlets, and the steelworks was able to supply outside customers as well as the NESCO stamping plants. During World War I, the company's plants operated at peak capacity when Granite City Steel contributed to U.S. defense by rolling the critically needed heavy plate steel for ships.

In 1961, Nicholas P. Veeder, president of Granite City Steel, was invited to address the American Newcomen Society at their St. Louis Dinner. This society is dedicated to honoring the lives, work, and contributions of those who founded and carried forward industrial enterprises in many fields. Its name memorializes the life and work of Thomas Newcomen (1663-1729), the British pioneer whose valuable contributions to the newly invented steam engine paved the way for the Industrial Revolution.

Veeder stated in his address, "Building the Foundations For Today's Growth, The Story of Granite City Steel Company, (1878-1961)," that by 1927, the steelworks "was shipping substantial tonnages of flat rolled steel to customers other than NESCO. In that year all of NESCO's steelmaking properties and assets were transferred to the Granite City Steel Company and our career as an independent corporation was underway."

Postcard, "Royal Granite Ware National Enameling Co., Granite City, Ill." $15

Hayward Niedringhaus became president of Granite City Steel in 1930. He kept the company alive by the conversion to continuous rolling. Hayward Niedringhaus died unexpectedly in the late 1940s and was succeeded by John N. Marshall, who transformed the company into a modern, integrated plant and, according to Veeder, "enabled us to profit from our specialization in flat rolled products."

The company became a division of National Steel Corporation in 1971, and has a reputation as one of the lowest-cost manufacturers of quality steel in this country.

Today, 3,900 men and women are employed at Granite City Steel. The following explains the commitment of the company's 1985 management committee: "Our business consists of producing a high-quality product at low cost, and delivering it to the customer at the right time — nothing more, nothing less."

The National Enameling and Stamping Company was sold to Knapp-Monarch in 1955. Hoover bought the companies in 1969 and sold the NESCO and Knapp-Monarch trade names to Crown Industries, Binghampton, New York, in 1979.

Manufacturers

Many companies' histories were similar to the St. Louis Stamping Company's, and some of the manufacturers were comparable in size, production, and progress. The following list of manufacturers is as complete as possible. Retailers and jobbers are included only when the manufacturers are unknown.

Albert Pick and Company, Chicago, Illinois. Wholesalers of supplies for hotels, restaurants, clubs, and institutions. Their 1926 catalog offered Lisk, Genuine Agate, El-an-ge, and domestic white wares from America's leading factories. Also offered was Czechoslovakian Elite and Austrian wares in olive green or brown with white linings.

Arrow paper label.

The Asception Company, New York. "Hospital Quality Enameled Ware," white with navy trim.

Atlantic Stamping Company, Rochester, New York.

Azurelite stamped mark.

Baltimore Stamping and Enameling Company, Baltimore, Maryland. Samson and Oriole Ware paper labels.

Banner Stamping Works. Aetna, American, Azure, Dresden, Iron Gray, Ivorine, Purity, Titan, and Whitecote. Manufactured vast quantities of labeled enamelware for Butler Brothers.

Barrows Savory Company, Philadelphia, Pennsylvania, 1850s. One of the first to enamel cast-iron cookware in the United States.

Belknap Hardware and Manufacturing Company, Louisville, Kentucky. Wholesale distributor of "Old Kentucky Home," among others. In 1840, W. B. Belknap founded House of Belknap, which later grew to a twelve-building, thirty-seven acre plant, located one block from the Ohio River for convenient shipping. Called W.B. Belknap & Company, 1860; W.B. Belknap & Co., Inc. 1880; Belknap Hardware and Manufacturing Company, 1907; and, as of 1985, Belknap, Inc. Longtime employee stated, "We never made enamelware here; we were wholesalers."

The Bellaire Enamel Company, Bellaire, Ohio. Beco Ware and Princess Ware on labels with pictures of long-legged birds.

Bellaire Stamping Company, Bellaire, Ohio, established October 16, 1871. Fire destroyed the building in 1890. A new plant was built in Harvey, Illinois, for porcelain enameling. Adopted eagle-in-circle trademark March 6, 1894. Ajax was their bluish gray, second-quality ware. It had a fourth coat and was recommended as superior to the three-coated ware, according to the February, 1900, price list. In 1900, fire destroyed the plant. June, 1902, a new factory was built in Terre Haute, Indiana, and was named Columbian Enameling and Stamping Company. Made Kapnerite, Columbian Enameled Ware, Columbian Enameled Steel Ware, and enameled steel advertising signs. The name was adopted from the 1893 Columbian Exposition in Chicago. In 1968, joined General Housewares Corporation Cookware Group, P. O. Box 4066, Terre Haute, Indiana 47804.

Belmont Stamping and Enameling Company, New Philadelphia, Ohio. High Grade Enameled Ware, Belmont Ware, Sanitare, and Tuscora.

Benham and Stoutenborough, 270-272 Pearl Street, New York. Wholesaler. Sold Agate Ware and Granite Ware. Also sold metal-trimmed and nickel-plated Granite Ware teapots in four styles, including ones with planished tin covers and Britannia handles and spouts.

Biddle Hardware Company. A 1910 catalog advertised El-an-ge Mottled Gray Enamel, Onyx, and Turquoise.

Bluestone Porcelain Enamel paper label. Dark blue and white mottled ware, "Easy to Clean as China."

Bonnie Blue, made in USA, 1923. Turquoise with white scallops and dots. Similar pieces have been found marked "Germany."

Bronson Supply Company, Cleveland, Ohio, and New York. Made "Never Break Enameled Steel" cooking utensils. Won Medal of Superiority at the American Institute of Manufacturers in New York, 1889.

Butler Brothers. Jobbers and wholesalers. Issued monthly, quarterly, and seasonal catalogs to merchants. Slogan was "Our Catalog Is Our Salesman." Registered "Our Drummer" trademark in 1886. Sold granite ware made by all the major companies in America, as well as imported ware. Now called City Products Corporation, Inc.

Canton Stamping and Enameling Company, Canton, Ohio, also known as C.S. & E. Company. French Gray Steelware, patented June 14, 1904. Pieces were given with purchase of Voigt's Crescent Milling Company products. Made gray only until the 1920s, when white became their leading color. Ivory with green was second. Also made pastels. After being sold to Federal Enameling and Stamping Company in 1953, the company was phased out and the plant was closed.

Cat's Eye Grey Steelware paper label.

Central Stamping Company, Newark, New Jersey, founded 1834. Headquarters in New York City. Made Agate Steelware, 1889; September 2, 1902; April 26, 1904; and November 8, 1904. Made Sterling Gray Enameled Ware; Dresden Aluminum Enameled Ware, patented 1892, 1903, 1904; Sterling on Enameled Ware Means the Same as Sterling on Silverware; Sterling White; Primo White; and Model. Also made Primo Grey Enameled Ware, September 2, 1902; April 25, 1904, and November 8, 1904. Primo Aluminum Enameled Ware, April, 1892; November 8, 1904. In 1931 was sold to Republic Metalware Company. Merged in 1944 with Lisk Manufacturing Company to form Lisk Savory Corporation.

Challenge paper label.

Chef-ette Enameled Ware Made in USA paper label.

Chrysolite is dark green with white vein marks and a white interior edged in deep blue. It won a Silver Medal and Diploma at the Paris World's Fair in 1900.

Cleveland Metal Products Company, 7608-7632 Platt Avenue, Cleveland, Ohio. October 18, 1919, and October 16, 1920, issues of *Saturday Evening Post* advertised True Blue and Alladin Enameled Steel.

Cleveland Stamping and Tool Company, Cleveland, Ohio. Made Lava and Volcanic Enameled Ware.

Columbian Enameling and Stamping Company, Terre Haute, Indiana. (*Also see* Bellaire Stamping Company history). Trademark was "C" encircling "E&S Co." Label with eagle appears on Amethyst and on olive-green-on-white ware. Made Hoosier Gray Ware — Extra Quality, Universal Practical Enamelware, Onyx World's Best, and Sanitrox Ware. Onyx came in a brown-and-white mottled and in solid white. Onyx Queen was shaded green on white with white interior. Domestic science authorities designed Onyx utensils. *Good Housekeeping Magazine* ad, June, 1924, offered Sanitrox eighteen-piece starter set for $15 postage prepaid. Claimed to be the largest exclusive manufacturers of enamelware in the world. The Depression posed particular hardships on granite ware companies. Columbian's production was vital to the economy of its community, and, in an effort to keep the plant open, management cut salaries and reduced profits. In 1934 four hundred and fifty out of five hundred production workers joined the A.F.L. The result was the third general strike in American history. The National Guard was called in to subdue the violence, and it was six months before differences were settled. The company made military mess kits for World War II. Made Willow Ware, Blue Onion, and Frontier Ware. Bought Fletcher Company in 1958. In 1966, imported French ware: Fanci Pans, decorated with paisley and houndstooth designs, and Normandy, the original line of imported cookware that launched the trend to full decoration.

Coonley Manufacturing Company, Cicero, Illinois. Made blue and white enamel.

Crunden-Martin Manufacturing Company, St. Louis, Missouri. Made Parrot Ware and Cru-Marco. Trademark: "C" over "M" enclosed in a circle. Old labels have six parrots; later labels have one or none. Company now makes plastic household items. This company was erroneously listed as Grunden-Martin in our first book.

Defiance Enameled Ware paper label. Kresge's catalog offered this ware for five and ten cents.

Dover Stamping and Manufacturing Company, 385 Putnam Avenue, Cambridge, Massachusetts. Advertised complete line of enamelwares and specialties, including gray mottled ware, white, blue and white, and all fancy colors. Also made stoves. Now a division of the Parkersburg Steel Company.

Enterprise Enamel Company, Bellaire, Ohio. Made Corona Enamel Ware and Daisy White. Came in plain colors and designs created by "a famous American artist." Used crown symbol on paper labels. Made a full line of household articles.

Farwell, Ozman, and Kirk. Wholesaler. Enamelware advertised in 1928 catalog. Pans given to merchants were labeled "L & G Mfg Co, Flint Gray Enamelware, Compliments of Farwell, Ozman, Kirk & Co."

Federal Enameling and Stamping Company, Pittsburgh, Pennsylvania. Labels: Iron City, Federal Metal Wares, and Federal. Advertised multicolor rose designs permanently fused into white enamel with black or red trim. In 1953, bought Canton Stamping and Enameling Company.

Fletcher Quality Porcelain Enamel Company, Dunbar (Charlestown), West Virginia. Labels: Kanawha on white ware with red trim, 1955; Acme, Fletcher Enamel Co, on gray ware. Made large quantities of step-on garbage cans, water pails, and outdoor grills. Sold to Columbian, 1958.

General Housewares Corporation Cookware Group, P.O. Box 4066, Terre Haute, Indiana 47804. Founded in 1968 as a result of mergers and acquisitions. Bought Columbian Enameling and Stamping Company same year. (*See* "What Happened to Granite Ware.") At present, the only manufacturer of granite ware in the United States. Label: GHC.

Geuder, Paeschke and Frey Company, Milwaukee, Wisconsin, founded in 1880. Manufacturers and jobbers. Trademark: Cream City in honor of the dairy industry. Began making porcelain enamelware in 1911. Made Tulip Ware. Discontinued consumer division in 1957 to concentrate on industrial and commercial products. This company was one of the most important manufacturers of kitchenwares in the United States.

Haberman Manufacturing Company, New York. One of six to merge and form the National Enameling and Stamping Company in 1899.

Haller Manufacturing Company, New Orleans, Louisiana. One of six to merge and form the National Enameling and Stamping Company in 1899.

Hardwick name embossed on ashtray.

Hero paper label.

Hibbard, Spencer, and Bartlett and Company, State Street Bridge, Chicago, Illinois. Jobbers who sold products of the major companies: Royal, NESCO, Adamant, Chrysolite, Nu Blu, Iris, and H.S.B. Co. — Revonoc. Imported white ware from Germany.

Ingram-Richardson Manufacturing Company, 11 West 42nd Street, New York. Factory located in Beaver Falls, Pennsylvania. Trademark: Porceliron. Made tabletops in a variety of styles, sizes, and patterns according to 1939 catalog. Tabletops were sold to manufacturers, who attached the legs.

Iron Clad Manufacturing Company, Cliff Street, New York, New York, established in 1850 by Robert Seaman. Made Ironclad, patented July 10, 1888, and Salamander Ware in 1893. The latter had an additional bottom made of copper to allow for free circulation of air in the air chamber thus formed. This prevented burning and injury to the vessel. Also made Hearthstone. One of the largest and oldest manufacturers of granite ware. When Robert Seaman died in 1904, his wife, Elizabeth Cochran (a famous journalist whose pen name was Nellie Bly), took over management of the company. Her photograph was distributed on Iron Clad advertising cards at the Pan-American Exposition in 1901. She was touted as the only woman in the world who personally managed an industry of such magnitude. Unfortunately, the company went bankrupt by the end of 1913. We hope it was not due to her management.

Jones Metal Products Company, West Lafayette, Ohio. Paper label states "Hospital and Surgical Ware."

Keen and Hagerty Manufacturing Company, Race, Ostend, Clements and Creek Streets, Baltimore, Maryland. Made Gray Flint Enameled Ware. Merged with five others to form NESCO in 1899.

Keystone Enamel Ware, American Process red label in diamond shape.

Kieckhefer Brothers, Milwaukee, Wisconsin. Merged with five other companies to form NESCO in 1899.

Lalance and Grosjean Manufacturing Company, Woodhaven, New York, established 1850 by Florian Grosjean and Charles Lalance. L & G became the largest and one of the most skilled manufacturers of metal stampings in the country. Made equipment for the government for four wars; Patent Agate Iron Ware, patented May 22, 1877; Opal Iron Ware; Crystal Steel Ware, patented June 5, 1883; Blue and White Enameled Ware; Blue and Blue Enameled Ware; White Enameled Ware; Agate Nickel-Steel Ware, Patent 1897; Flint Grey Enameled Ware; Enamel Cooking and Sanitary Wares; El-an-ge; Pearl Agate Ware; and Regal Steel Ware. They also made Sears, Roebuck and Company's Peerless Grey Ware. Their trademarks were burned in the enamel. In 1901, L & G began using the Blue Label in addition to others. The 1903 catalog offered white cuspidors decorated with floral designs.

Leader, Pure Enameled Ware USA label.

Leyden, Triple Coated Marbleized Blue and White on Steel, label.

Lisk Manufacturing Company, Clifton Springs, New York, founded in 1889. *Harper's Magazine Advertiser*, 1904, stated that Lisk guaranteed four coats on each piece. An ad in 1905 guaranteed the Imperial Gray Enamel Steel Roaster for ten years. Lisk was located in Canandaigua, New York, according to their 1923 catalog. Merged with Republic Metalware Company in 1944 to become the Lisk Savory Corporation. Famous for the Lisk Self-Basting Roaster. Colors: robin's-egg blue, turquoise, cadet blue, cobalt blue, white, brown, gray, and dark green.

Lisk Savory Corporation, formed in 1944, with the merger of the Lisk Manufacturing Company and the Republic Metalware Company. Purchased the U.S. Stamping Company, 1956.

Lustron Corporation, Columbus, Ohio. One of five companies that built porcelain steel prefabricated homes for World War II veterans. Lustron was financed by government funds through the Reconstruction Finance Corporation. Local labor assembled the enameled walls and roofs on cement foundations. The endeavor was not successful. There was a shortage of steel and it was not a sound financial venture. Recently a Lustron home was advertised for sale for five thousand dollars. It sold and was dismantled and moved.

Manning-Bowman and Company, Cromwell, Connecticut, established in 1859 by Thaddeus Manning and Robert Bowman. Was founded by Thomas Manning and son in 1849. One of the oldest firms in the housewares business. Refinanced by the Meriden Britannia Company in 1872 and moved to Meriden. Trademarks: Patent Perfection Granite Iron Ware Girdles the Globe, Decorated Pearl Agateware, and Seamless Ivory Enameled Ware with Planished Copper Rim. August, 1945, sold to Bersted Manufacturing Company, Chicago. This company was purchased by McGraw-Edison in 1948. Name survives as Manning-Bowman Division of the McGraw-Edison Company of Booneville, Missouri.

Page from 1885 Manning-Bowman catalog.

1885 Manning-Bowman catalog, pages 48 and 49.

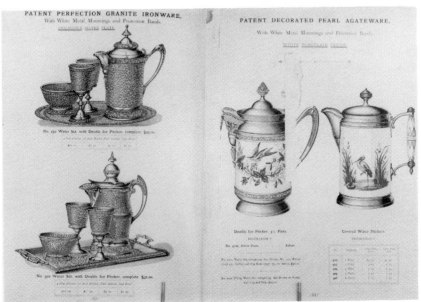

Pages 50 and 51.

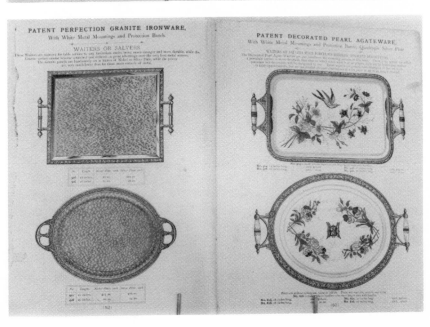

Pages 52 and 53.

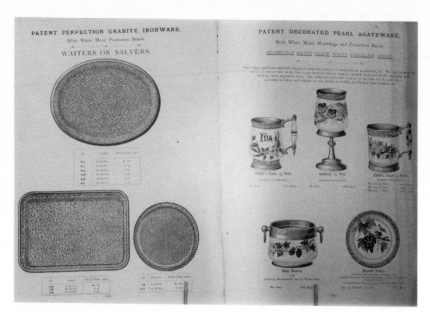

Pages 54 and 55.

Pages 56 and 57.

Pages 58 and 59.

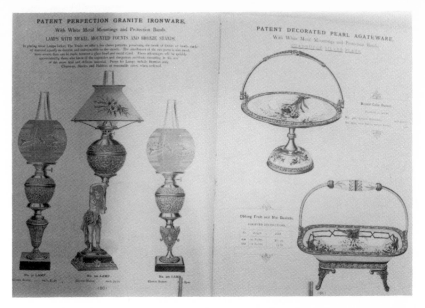

Pages 60 and 61.

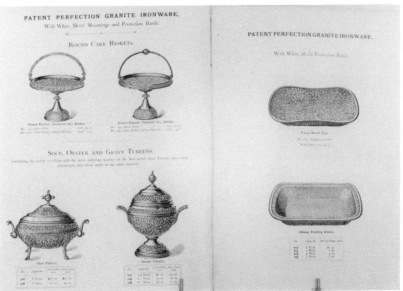

Pages 62 and 62 A.

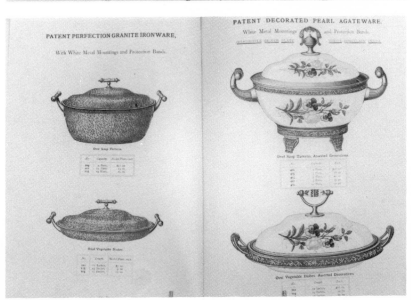

Pages 62 B and 63.

Pages 64 and 65.

Pages 66 and 67. "Sleeping and Parlor Car Spittoons," advertised to be hand painted.

Pages 68 and 69.

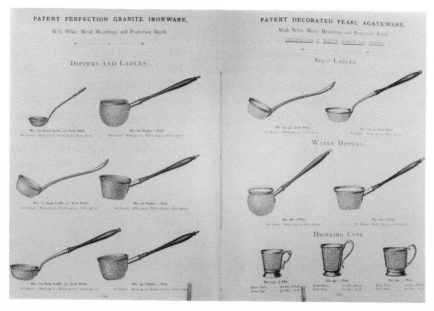

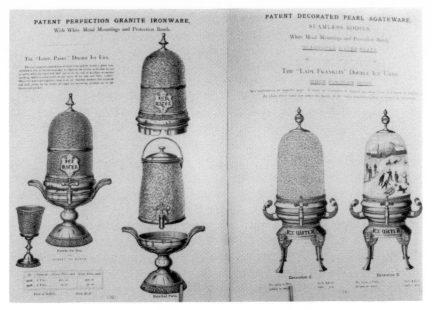

Pages 70 and 71.

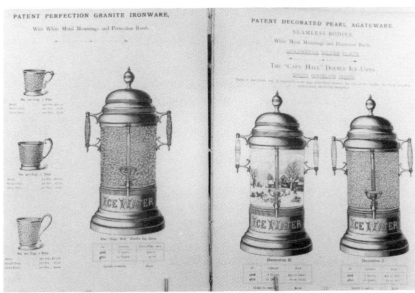

Pages 72 and 73.

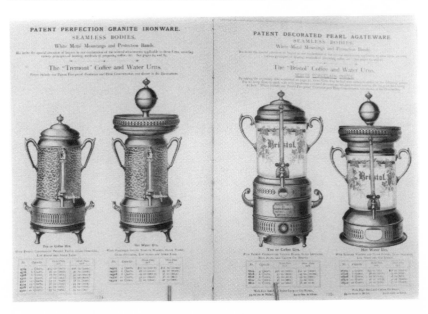

Pages 74 and 75.

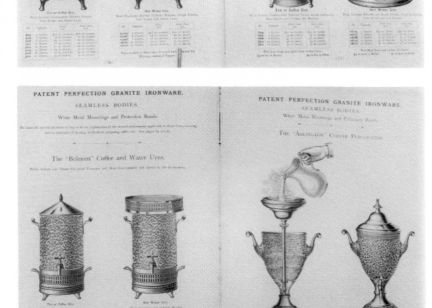

Marietta Hollow-Ware and Enameling Company, Marietta, Pennsylvania.

Matthai-Ingram Company, Baltimore, Maryland. Merged with five other companies to form NESCO in 1899. Made Greystone Enameled Ware.

Maxwell's Peerless Triple Coated Ware, label.

Montgomery Ward and Company, Chicago, Illinois. Retail distributor for a large variety of colors, quality, and sets. Sold granite ware by mail. The first mail-order service by Montgomery Ward was in 1872. When the Rural Free Delivery Service began in 1896, mail-order firms became the largest customers of the Post Office. Mobil Corporation acquired Montgomery Ward in 1976. The company plans to phase out its catalog sales division by the end of 1986.

Moore Enameling and Manufacturing Company, West Lafayette, Ohio. Made La Fayette Quality Ware.

Mosaic Triple Coated R.P. Ware, label.

National Enameling and Stamping Company (NESCO), formed in 1899 with the merger of the St. Louis Stamping Company, the Haberman Manufacturing Company, Haller Manufacturing Company, Keen and Hagerty, Kieckhefer Brothers, and Matthai-Ingram. In 1955, sold to Knapp-Monarch Company of St. Louis, which sold to the Hoover Company in 1969. Hoover sold NESCO and Knapp-Monarch trade names to Crown Industries, Binghampton, New York, in 1979. Made Nesco Royal Granite Enameled Ware, Royal Granite Steelware, Pure Greystone Enameled Ware, and Diamond Enameled Steelware. First NESCO label was paper, on which was printed a gray kettle. This was the trademark of the St. Louis Stamping Company.

The New England Enameling Company, Middletown, Connecticut, and Portland, Connecticut. Labels: New England Quality Ware, Made in USA; Ideal, and N.E.E.Co. The company was the exclusive agent for the German-made Paragon Lion Brand Enameled Ware.

Nichthauser and Levy, 96 Beekman Street, New York. In 1904, they advertised kerosene oil stoves with reservoirs of seamless enameled ware that made them leakproof.

Norvell Shapleigh (originally Shapleigh Hardware; Norvell joined the firm in the early 1900s). Wholesalers of Polly Prim, Shamrock Ware, Blue Diamond Ware, White Diamond Ware, Sage, Bluebelle Ware, Thistle Ware, Stewart Rozwood Enameled Ware, and Dixie Ware.

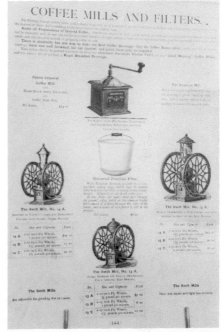

Page 144. "For filtering through textile fabric, coffee should be ground to a granulated powder — not merely broken into coarse grains, nor yet reduced to the fineness of flour — but resembling to the touch that of fine Indian bean.

"Avoid all Preparations of Ground Coffee. Should you chance to find a pure article, its most delicate properties will already have been lost by exposure; and, in case you see the pulverized brand in air tight packages, look out for rancid and bitter qualities generated in this most unscientific and objectionable method of preparing coffee for sale.

"There is absolutely but one way to make the Best Coffee Beverage — buy the Coffee Beans often (unless you do your own roasting), fresh and well browned, but not charred, and grind them only as required.

"Then follow closely the printed directions for using our Universal Porcelain Textile Filter, or our "Good Morning" Coffee Maker, and you cannot fail to produce a Royal Breakfast Beverage."

Pacific Hardware and Steel Company, made Blulite Enameled Ware.

Polar Ware Company, Sheboygan, Wisconsin. Established in the early 1920s by W. J. Vollrath. In 1924 made all white ware. In 1928 made Polar Colored Enamel Ware in coral red, jade green, powder blue, and canary yellow.

Prizer-Ware, P. O. Box 1382, Reading, Pennsylvania. Made Dutch Tulip porcelain cast iron in white with blue tulips.

Reed Manufacturing Company, Newark, New York. Famous for its Reed Sanitary Self-Basting Roaster, embossed Reed. Colors of turquoise, white with dark trim, white with floral pattern, white with black speckles, dark gray, and brown.

Republic Metalware Company, established in 1905, formerly Sidney Shepard and Company of Buffalo, New York. In 1931 bought Central Stamping Company. Merged with the Lisk Manufacturing Company in 1944 to form the Lisk Savory Corporation. Made Savory in 1909. Also made Magnolia, Hearthstone, Niagara, and Steel Gray Enamelware. Used Handihook Pot Cover paper label, marked "Patented December 17, 18, 1912."

Republic Stamping and Enameling Company, Canton, Ohio, founded June, 1904. Made Old Hampshire Gray; Old English Enameled Ware; Old English Gray Ware, Purity and Quality, U.S. Patent June 1904; and Republic Ware. Colors: white with ebony, ivory with jade green, and ivory with mandarin red. Sold to Ekco Products Company, 1952. Enamelware discontinued.

Roesch, Bellville, Illinois. Items such as tabletops, stove doors, and reservoirs were sent to Roesch, enameled to specification, and returned to the factories to be assembled.

St. Louis Stamping Company, St. Louis, incorporated in 1866 by William F. and Frederick G. Niedringhaus. The earliest patent date we have is June 9, 1874, for Granite Iron Ware. In 1899, merged with five other companies to form NESCO. (*See* "History of The St. Louis Stamping Company.")

Saks Stamping Company, Long Island City, New York. Made Service Hospital Enamel Ware in gray with dark trim.

Savory, Incorporated, 90 Alabama Street, Buffalo, New York. Made porcelain enamelware on Armco (American Rolling Mill Company) ingot iron.

Sears, Roebuck and Company, Chicago, established in 1893. Retail distributors for True Blue Enamel Steelware, Acme Ironstone Enamel Ware, Eclipse Ironstone Enamel Ware, Imperial Stove Hollow Ware, and Peerless Grey Ware.

Shapleigh Hardware Company, St. Louis, Missouri, established 1843. Became Norvell Shapleigh in early 1900s.

Sidney Hollowware Company. One of the early manufacturers of enameled cast iron.

Sidney Shepard, Bath, New York, 1836. Became Sidney Shepard and Company when Thadeus Crane became a partner in 1838. Changed name to Republic Metalware Company, 1905.

Standard Lighting Company, 153 Seneca Street, Cleveland, Ohio. Made The Vigil stove, lamp, and lantern of enamel and nickel plating.

Standard Manufacturing Company, Pittsburgh, Pennsylvania. One of the first companies to make enameled iron cooking pots. Became a major producer of plumbing fixtures.

Two letterheads indicating that the St. Louis Stamping Company and Manning-Bowman & Co. shared the same salesroom at 57 Beekman St., New York, in 1880. **$15 each**
"Granite Iron Ware" 1889 magazine ad. Rare. The St. Louis Stamping Company did not advertise a great deal in magazines, although they advertised more than any other company with trade cards, trays, fans and pictures. **$15**

Steel Gray Guaranteed Ware, patented June 14, 1904.

Stewart Stamping Company, Ash Avenue, Moundsville, West Virginia. In 1901, William C. Stewart set up shop across from the United States Stamping Company and supplied them with frit and milled enamels. Built three-story plant in 1905 with materials salvaged from the St. Louis World's Fair. Began enameling iron bedsteads that were being made in the state prison nearby. Stewart purchased steel shapes from the U.S.S. Company and persuaded prison officials to allow prisoners to enamel cooking utensils. This ended with a change in the prison administration. Stewart then bought some of the prison equipment, enlarged his plant, bought shapes from the U.S.S. Company, and made Stewart Ware. This ware was a diffused turquoise blue with yellow and pink flowers. Some was stamped "Moundsville W. Va, Stewart." Only a few pieces remain. A lawsuit filed in 1910 by the United States Stamping Company culminated with a takeover of the Stewart Stamping Company.

Stransky and Company, 9 to 15 Murray Street, New York, New York. Imported Stransky Steel Ware, Quadruple Coated, The Ware That Wears.

Stuart-Peterson Company, Broad and Noble Streets, Philadelphia, Pennsylvania. One of the first companies to enamel cast iron. Won First Premium at the International Exhibition, 1876. Patented October 3, 1871; reissued April 9, 1872.

The Strong Manufacturing Company, Sebring, Ohio. Early catalog indicates that the company moved from Bellaire, Ohio. Everglade, Oceanic, Concord, and Emerald were made in Bellaire. Strong claimed to have originated blended enamelware. Made Blue Blend, Alice Blue, Concord, Ripe Concord Grape, Everglade, Emerald Ware, and Oceanic.

The Success Enameling and Stamping Company, St. Louis. Made Dixie Ware, distributed by Norvell Shapleigh.

United States Stamping Company, Ash Avenue, Moundsville, West Virginia. Trademark: "U.S.S." Founded in 1901 by investors who built scanty sheds to cover equipment and brought in experienced enamelers from Bellaire, Ohio. Bought iron shapes from Bellaire and other companies. September, 1902, began enameling. In 1903, enlarged facilities and installed press and tool and die equipment to make their own shapes. By 1910, plant was greatly enlarged. Purchased Stewart Enameling and Chemical Plants and renamed them The United States Stamping Company Plant #2. In 1925, produced thirty-six hundred different items, including hospital and sickroom supplies. Installed one of the first continuous enameling furnaces in the United States. Sold to Lisk Savory in 1956. Plant closed in the 1970s. The buildings were destroyed by fire in 1982. Made U.S. Bisque, U.S. Ivory, and U.S. Opal.

Vollrath Company, Sheboygan, Wisconsin. Established by Jacob J. Vollrath, 1874. One of the early large manufacturers of enamelware. Vollrath learned "wet" enameling from friends in Germany. He began enameling stamped sheet steel utensils in 1892. In the early 1900s, made Duchess, a splashy design of blue daubs on a web of blue, cocoa, and white. Collectors call it Turtle, Chickenwire, or Tortoise. The company was one of the leaders in perfecting a good white enamel, which was difficult. Made colored ware to harmonize with the kitchen in the late 1920s. Made Town and Terrace and Provencial Ware. In 1962, discontinued manufacturing enamelware, according to Carl P. Vollrath, great-grandson of Jacob J. Vollrath. Carl P. Vollrath was vice-president and secretary of the company in 1980. The company now manufactures stainless steel utensils.

West Mansfield Enameling Company, West Mansfield, Ohio.

Page from early wholesale catalog showing the "Stuart, Peterson & Company's Enameled Maslin Kettle and Round and Oval Boilers, Tinned or Enameled." Label: "International Exhibition 1876, First Premium, Stuart, Peterson & Co.'s Enameled Ware, The only Enamel that stood all the Chemical Tests applied by the German Government Experts. The ingredients composing this Pure Enamel, are so difficult to fuse, that they must be applied to the hollow-ware in iron ovens kept at a white heat, such heat as would dissolve and evaporate lead or other poisonous metallic enamels. Double Check Bail. Patented, October 3d, 1871. Reissued, April 9, 1872."

"Samson, Baltimore Stamping and Enameling Co., Baltimore, MD."

Labels and Trademarks

Labels and trademarks are useful aids when tracing the history of factories. For instance, the St. Louis Stamping Company marked its ware with "Granite Iron Ware" from the 1860s until 1899, when it merged with five other companies to form the National Enameling and Stamping Company.

The pictures in this chapter are arranged alphabetically by the manufacturer, when known, or by the trade name. The only exception is the St. Louis Stamping Company, for which the merging companies follow.

Paper labels are sold to collectors of advertising as well as of granite ware. They range in price from one dollar to fifteen dollars. The value of the piece of enamelware is increased when the original label is still affixed; however, there is no guarantee that a label has not been applied to facilitate a ready sale.

"Safety, Durability, Quality, ORIOLE WARE, B S & E Co."

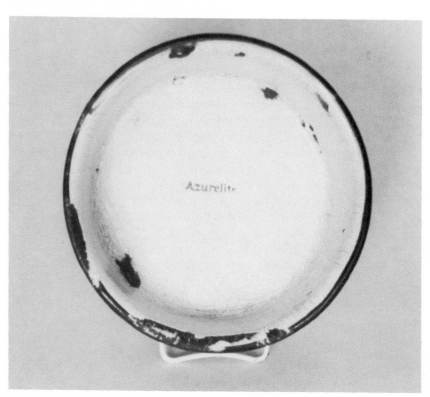

"Azurelite."

"TITAN ENAMELED WARE, Banner Stamping Works."

"CATS-EYE GREY STEEL WARE."

"IRON GRAY ENAMELWARE, Banner Stamping Wks."

"Sterling Gray Enameled Ware, The Central Stamping Company, N.Y."

"TUSCORA, The Belmont Stamping and Enameling Co., New Philadelphia, Ohio."

"PRIMO Aluminum Enameled Ware,
The Central Stamping Company, N.Y.,
Patented Sept 2, 1902, April 26, 1904, Nov
8, 1904."

"Challenge Porcelain Enamel Ware."

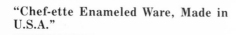

"DRESDEN Aluminum Enameled
Ware."

"Chef-ette Enameled Ware, Made in
U.S.A."

"Columbian Enameling & Stamping Co. Terre Haute, Indiana, HOOSIER GRAY."

"The Cleveland Stamping & Tool Co. Manufacturers of LAVA & VOLCANIC Enameled Ware, Cleveland, O."

"DRESDEN Enameled Ware, Extra Coated Aluminum, The Central Stamping Company, N.Y."

"COLUMBIAN MADE, CESCO, Official Registered Seal, New Improved Porcelain on Steel ENAMELEDWARE."

"Columbian Enameling & Stamping Co., Inc., Terre Haute, Ind., COLUMBIAN MADE."

"Parrot Ware, Mottled Gray Enamel, Cleans Like China." *Note:* Label with six parrots is older than with one or none.

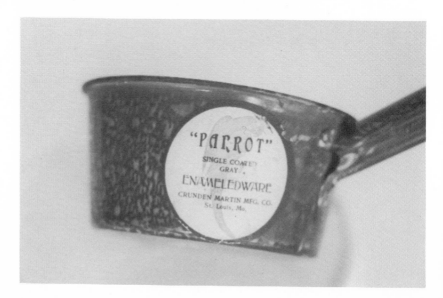

One-parrot label.

"DEFIANCE ENAMELED WARE, Quality Durability Special."
"DEFIANCE ENAMELED WARE, Quality and Durability Guaranteed, Made in USA."

"PARROT Single Coated Gray Enameledware, Crunden Martin Mfg. Co. St. Louis, Mo."

"FRENCH GRAY, CS & E Co."

"Crumarco Enameled Ware, Crunden Martin Mfg. Co. St. Louis."

"GENERAL STEEL WARES LTD."

"FEDERAL."

"CREAM CITY WARE, G&P."

"HERO Enameled Ware, Crown Bail
Holder Holds Bail Up — Keeps It Cool."

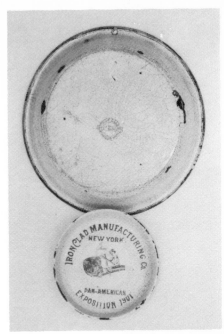

"IRON CLAD Enameled Ware, Best Quality."
"Iron Clad Manufacturing Co. New York, Pan-American Exposition 1901."

"American Process KEYSTONE Ware."

"JONES Specialized."
"JONES Specialized, The Jones Metal Products Company, Hospital Surgical Ware, Irrigator, West Lafayette, Ohio."
"ARMCO, Porcelain Enamel on Ingot Iron."

"EXTRA AGATE Nickel Steel Ware, L & G Mfg Co."

"EL-AN-GE MOTTLED GRAY WARE."

"AGATE Nickel Steel Ware, L & G Mfg Co."

"EXTRA AGATE Nickel Steel Ware, L & G Mfg Co."

"AGATE Nickel Steel Ware, L & G Mfg Co., 40 Years World's Standard."

"EL-AN-GE Mottled Gray Ware."

"WHITE ENAMELED WARE With Blue Border, L & G Mfg Co."

"LISK."

"EL-AN-GE Mottled Steel Ware."

"LEADER."

"LaFayette Quality Ware, The Moore Enameling & Mfg. Company, West Lafayette, Ohio."

"NEW ENGLAND Quality Ware, N.E.E. Co."

"PURITY Enameled Ware, Pat Oct 9, 1894, Pat July 21, 1896."

"Handihook Pot Cover, R.M. Co, Chicago, Buffalo, New York."

"Made in Poland."

"Republic Ware."

"Old English Enameled Ware, Republic Stamping & Enameling Co., Canton, Ohio."

"Old English Gray Ware, RS&E CO."

"Old Hampshire Gray Certified, The Republic S-E Co., Canton, O. USA."

"OLD STYLE GRANITE WARE."

"SAGE WARE, St. Louis."

"GRANITE IRON WARE, Pat Oct 9, 94 and July 3, 93."

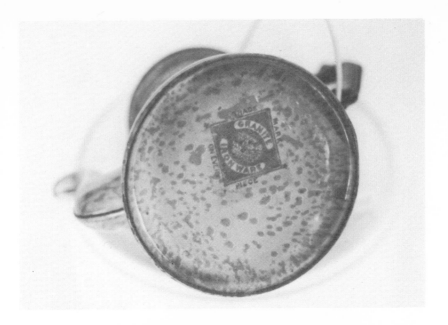

"GRANITE IRON WARE."

"GRANITE IRON WARE, Trade Mark On Every Piece."

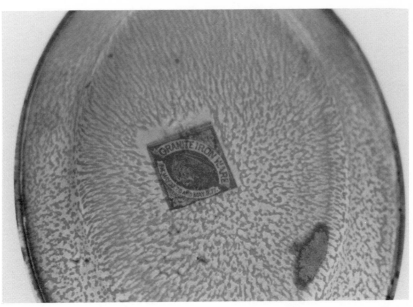

"PATENT ROYAL STEEL WARE, Pat. July 21, 1896, July 19, 1898, Sept 12, 1899."

"GRANITE IRON WARE, Pat May 30, 76 and May 8, 77." Note: Early date for the St. Louis Stamping Company.

"GRANITE STEEL WARE, Kieckhefer Twin Match Safe."

"NESCO ROYAL GRANITE STEEL
WARE, Patented Oct 9, 1895, July 1, 189 ,
Sept 20, 1896, July 19, 1898, Sept 12, 1899."

"ROYAL GRANITE STEEL WARE."

"GRANITE NESCO STEEL WARE."

"NESCO PURE GREYSTONE ENAM-
ELED WARE, Patented July 20, 1909,
Dec 3, 1912."

"NESCO."

"DIAMOND ENAMELED STEEL WARE NESCO, Patented Oct. 9, 1894, July 21, 1896, Sept 29, 1896, July 19, 1898, Sept 12, 1899." These patent dates are earlier than the Nesco merger.

"HABERMAN'S STEEL ENAMELED WARE, ROUND SALT BOX." The Haberman Manufacturing Company, New York, merged with the St. Louis Stamping Company and four other companies, including Kieckhefer Brothers of Milwaukee, Wisconsin to form NESCO in 1899.

"ROYAL GRANITE ENAMELED WARE."

"NESCO."

"SAVORY."

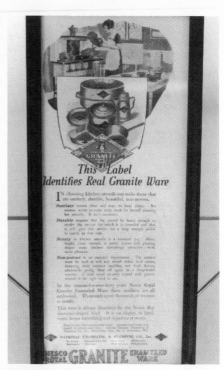

**"NESCO ROYAL GRANITE ENAM-
ELED WARE."**

"SERVICEABLE ENAMEL WARE."

**"ROYAL GRANITE ENAMELED
WARE, Nesco."**

Royal Granite Steel Ware tray, Evelyn Welch collection. $350
Photograph: Perry L. Struse, Jr.

Manning-Bowman Statue of Liberty cof-feepot designed to commemorate unveiling of statue, October 28, 1886, Courtesy Jay and Joan Smith. $295
Photograph: Perry L. Struse, Jr.

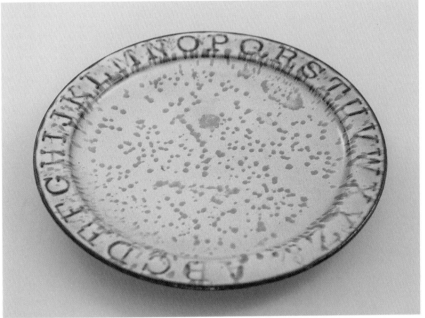

St. Louis Stamping Co. lettered plate, Evelyn Welch collection. $400
Photograph: Perry L. Struse, Jr.

Rare 2¼″ biscuit cutter, courtesy Brenda Hutto. Photograph: Perry L. Struse, Jr.

Lisk salesman's sample roaster with roasting rack and lid, courtesy Marnette Kilburn. **$195** Photograph: Perry L. Struse, Jr.

Columbian Enameling and Stamping Co. centennial souvenir piece, Evelyn Welch collection. **$45** Photograph: Perry L. Struse, Jr.

These lavabos are American made and difficult to find, probably because plumbing replaced them. However, they are still used in some parts of Europe. The font hangs on the wall and has a spigot to use to draw water into a basin, which can be attached to the wall or set on a table. **$300**

Ironclad Manufacturing Co. commemorative ashtray, Evelyn Welch collection. **$125** Photograph: Perry L. Struse, Jr.

Pedestal bowl. **$95**
Salt shaker, 2½″. **Heirloom**
Sugar bowl. **$200**

Lavabo. **$300**

Toy kitchen utensils, still in original packaging. **$300**

Double boiler, lid missing. **$35**
Coffeepot, Georges Briard. **$25**
Green roaster. **$45**
Pie pan, mottled, 10″. **$25**
Percolator. **$35**
Teakettle, "Wrought Iron Range Co., St. Louis, MO." **$75**

This handmade primitive stood atop a New Hampshire barn for many years, as evidenced by the damage to the enamel body. The handmade sheet-iron rooster was custom enameled in gray, and his comb and beak were painted. The hand-wrought iron directional was painted barn red. **$375**

"No country store would be complete without a display of early granite ware," states Marcia Brown. She and her husband Dell have collected early Americana and advertising for twenty-five years. She is pictured in a room in their home.

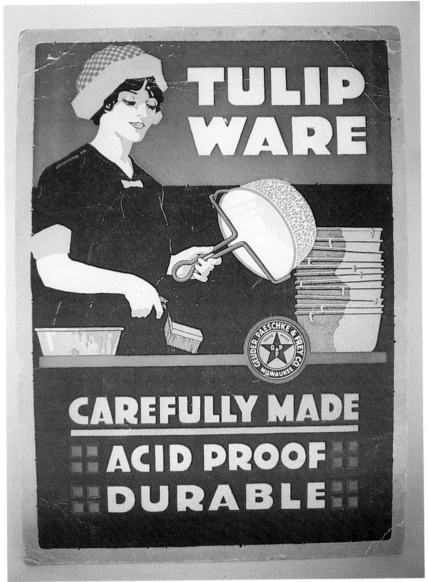

"Geuder, Pacsche & Frey" store card showing woman holding pan with tongs.
$38

Dutch Cleanser enameled sign. $250

Life-size NESCO lady store display. $50

"Dolly's Favorite, Cast Range, A Complete Range for Little Girls, The Favorite Stove and Range Co., Piqua, Ohio," featured in 1915 catalog. "It has good fire box and flues and will boil and bake the same as a large range. It has a lid holder, towel rail and lid lifter." Oven with rack measures 6½x7½x5″. This gray enameled toy stove is museum quality. It measures 23¾″ high, 18⅞″ long, and 10⅞″ wide. Two of the three stovepipe sections were removed for the photograph. **$2,900**

1984 Annual Holiday Table Settings event, sponsored by the McHenry Museum Guild, McHenry Museum, Modesto, California.

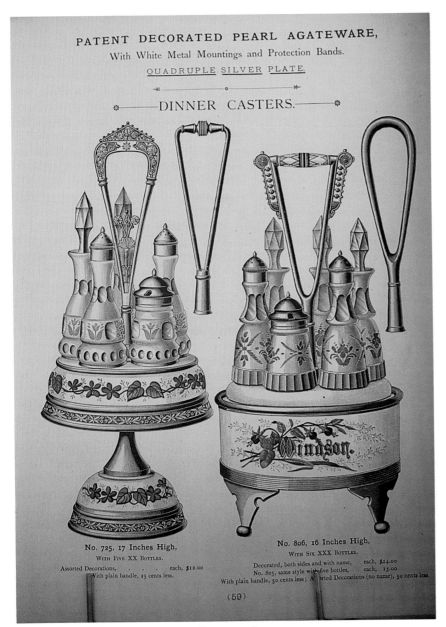

Manning-Bowman catalog, 1885, dinner casters.

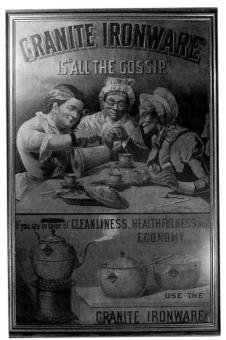

"Granite Ironware" advertising picture, linen-backed, 27½"x40½". Rare. **$3,000**

Manning-Bowman catalog, 1885, water server and goblet.

Enameled fobs. **$100**
Stickpins. **$50**
Cards. **$15**

Jean Phillips' floral arrangement complements the granite ware in her country home.

Enameled tabletop in 1920s style. **$125**

Life Saver enameled sign. Rare. **$350**

"OCEANIC, The Strong Manufacturing
Co. Bellaire, Ohio."
"CONCORD."

"EMERALD WARE, The Strong Manufacturing Co., Bellaire, Ohio."
"EVERGLADE."

"TIP TOP."

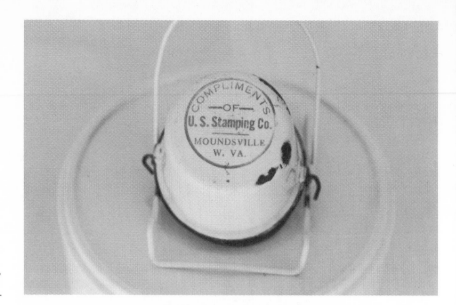

"Compliments of U.S. Stamping Co.,
Moundsville, W.VA."

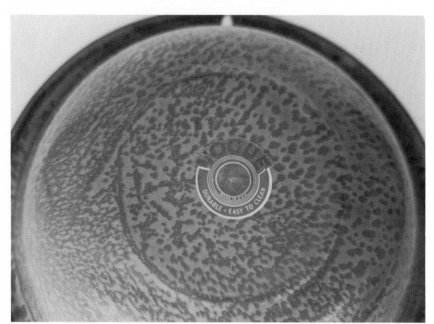

"VOGUE, Modern Design, Made in
USA."

"Vollrath, Since 1874."
"VOLLRATH, Original and Exclusive
Manufacturers of Vollrath Ware."

How It Was Made

After our first book was published, we received many letters from collectors who wanted to know more about how granite ware was made. So we delved into this aspect with some vigor when we began this book. We researched trade journals, catalogs, encyclopedias, and patents, and we contacted people who could give us firsthand information.

We were extremely fortunate in personally interviewing Merlin H. Whitehead, who worked in the porcelain enameling industry for more than thirty years. Whitehead graduated as a ceramic engineer from the University of Illinois and began his career in 1938 with the National Enameling and Stamping Company (NESCO, once the St. Louis Stamping Company), Granite City, Illinois.

Whitehead became lab foreman after working his way up from the mill room. He was hired as a ceramic engineer by the Canton Stamping Enameling Company in 1939. After serving as a colonel in the Army during World World II, he returned to Canton as superintendent.

Canton was sold to the Federal Enameling and Stamping Company, and Whitehead worked for Federal in McKees Rock, Pennsylvania, before he became superintendent of the Columbian Enameling and Stamping Company in Terre Haute, Indiana. He also worked as ceramic engineer for Columbian. In 1968, he retired, but returned to Columbian in 1972 as director of research and development. Since his subsequent retirement in 1976, he has consulted in Taiwan for the Ferro Industrial Products Enamel Company.

Whitehead explained the step-by-step process of making granite ware and loaned us valued personal photographs, old advertisements, salary schedules, and historical data about company's labor problems, mergers, misfortunes, and experiments such as the Lustron enameled homes. Whitehead brought the industry to life with observations and highlights of its leaders and pioneers. The following comes from our interview with Merlin Whitehead.

Dark blue centennial souvenir roaster. This is a good example of "speckled" ware, a popular form of decorating granite ware. Traffic manager and Merlin H. Whitehead, *right*, pictured at Columbian's One Hundredth Anniversary Open House in the enameling department. *Note:* The watch fob of the lower left in the photograph is an 1893 Columbian Exposition souvenir, "ONYX, WORLD'S BEST."

GWII: *What is the difference between what is commonly called porcelain enamel and "baked-on" enamel?*

Whitehead: Porcelain enamel is made of inorganic substances and is heated to temperatures of over 1,500°F. It is glass fused onto a metal base. All granite ware is porcelain enamel. Baked-on enamel is made of organic materials. Refrigerator exteriors are coated with "baked-on" enamel, and paint is made of organic materials.

Porcelain enamels will withstand much higher temperatures than any organic coating without burning off or discoloring, and they are more resistant to weathering and chemical attack. Even so, porcelain enamel is not indestructible and, although just about every kind of kitchen utensil was made of granite ware, it was not the best material for some things.

For example, granite ware skillets were not suited for the high setting of electrical or gas burners. Sometimes, the American housewife literally had a "burner." Asian and European enameled cooking utensils had a greater life expectancy because they were not subjected to such intense heat.

GWII: *Several accounts claim that granite ware got its name because it was made of ground-up granite. Is this true?"*

Whitehead: No. Granite was never ground up to make granite ware. The three main ingredients of enamel are quartz, feldspar, and borax. Appreciable amounts of soda ash, potassium, or sodium nitrate and flourspar, among a long list of other minerals, were added. The rock, granite, is composed of quartz and feldspar, but it also contains some black mica (biotite) and, less commonly, hornblende.

GWII: *A NESCO ad in the July, 1914,* Good Housekeeping *read, "The enamel is made with the real granite — that's part of our secret which makes the ware so hard, smooth and non-porous." Is this what we now term a misleading ad?"*

Whitehead: Definitely. It's catchy but untrue."

GWII: *Where do you think the name came from?*

Whitehead: People in the trade refer to the enameled hollowwares of all companies as granite ware. It is a generic term.

The St. Louis Stamping Company patented the trademark "Granite Iron Ware." When steel replaced iron in the production of granite ware, it was only natural to delete "Iron" from the name. The Niedringhaus Brothers founded a city in Illinois purposely for the location of their factories and named it Granite City. When they merged with five major companies to form the National Enameling and Stamping Company, they kept the name "Granite" and called the product "Royal Granite Enameled Ware."

GWII: *Iron and aluminum are also enameled. Why is steel the most popular?*

Whitehead: Steel is the ideal metal base for granite ware. It is strong, yet malleable. Cast iron was enameled much before steel, but it was hard to get good castings, and the weight was a problem.

Aluminum melts at a lower temperature than steel, and high temperatures are needed to fuse enamel on metal. Aluminum enamels at about 975°F.; steel at about 1,475 to 1,500°F. Aluminum is also softer and dents more readily. And where there are dents, enamel chips.

GWII: *Isn't it important that the enamel and the steel expand and contract at the same time so that the enamel will not chip and crack?*

Whitehead: Of course. The enamels must be compounded in such a manner that their expansion characteristics are compatible with the expansion characteristics of the steel, both during the firing process and ultimately when used in the cooking process. The usual result of incompatibility is cracking, crazing, or chipping (not impact chipping — heating and coating chipping).

The poor enameler could do nothing but weep or curse. The steel he got was what he used. The kitchenware manufacturers made up such an infinitesimal portion of the market that our needs or desires were largely ignored by the steel manufacturers.

GWII: *How were the steel shapes made?*

Whitehead: Before World War II, steel ingots were hot-rolled into thin coils. After World War II, steel was cold-rolled because certain ingredients for hot-rolled steel were not available.

The blanks were cut from the coils into various shapes on a blanking press. Round-tapered shapes and a few oval-tapered shapes, such as dish-pans, could be drawn in multiples, but when they came off the draw press, they were stuck together from the 250 tons of pressure exerted by the big press. All other shapes were placed on the draw press and drawn individually.

Canton Stamping and Enameling Company, 1946. The Processes of Making a Dishpan. **Merlin H. Whitehead weighing chemicals to make a testing solution for pickling room controls.**

Removing wrinkles by means of the spinning lathe.

Worker dipping pan in dip tank and catching the white enamel spattered by the brush. Note stream of enamel running in the trough and the roller pressing the bristles down to spatter the enamel.

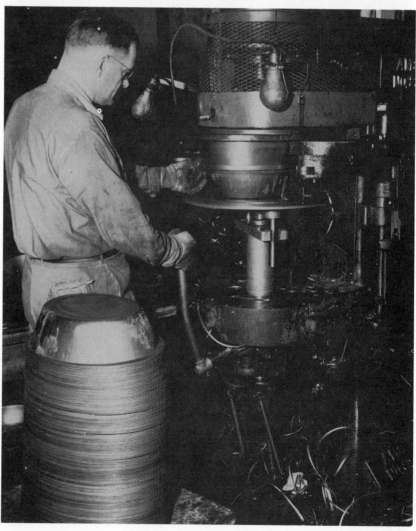

Trimming lathe knives cut the edge of a dishpan while on the other side of the lathe, a beading wheel turns the bead.

Workers preparing to rinse baskets of wares in the pickling department, where the steel is cleaned before enameling.

Enameling ground-coated dishpans.

Pans that have been dried over gas flames in the dryer are being removed from the slotted conveyor and stacked in crates.

GWII: *How were multiple pieces separated?*

Whitehead: After the blanks were shaped on the draw press, they were put on the spinning lathe to take out the wrinkles, and that just automatically separated them.

GWII: *What was the next step?*

Whitehead: The shape was then put on a trimming lathe. While the piece spun on the lathe, knives cut the edges and, at the same time, a beading wheel turned the bead to make a rim, as in the case of a dishpan.

The metal shapes were completely assembled before going to the Pickling Department. Spouts, handles, and lips were attached. Seams were riveted or welded together.

GWII: *Did the company make its own parts — spouts, ears, handles, bails?*

Whitehead: We did — right there at the plant. Except for intricate teakettle spouts or pieces that would cost too much to make the tools needed to make the parts. We saved money by purchasing the parts from a German enameling company if we only needed a few thousand pieces.

GWII: *Were teapots and coffeepots ever made all in one piece with the spout part of the original form?*

Whitehead: In the old days, it was impractical to draw forms because the steel was not capable of withstanding that pressure, so the pieces were rolled and welded at the seams. When World War II efforts brought about a tremendous increase in the quality of the steel, we were able to draw forms never before possible and we were able to draw the forms in one piece.

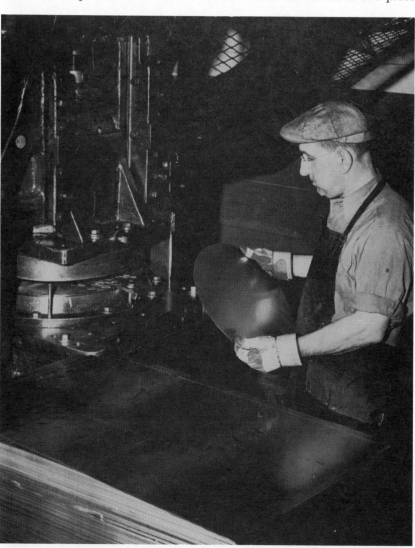

Worker cutting blanks for a dishpan on a blanking press using a blanking die.

GWII: *What is the Pickling Department?*

Whitehead: That is where the steel is cleaned. It had to be cleaned to prepare it for enameling. Steel is soiled when it comes from the steel mill, and the processing adds more soil. Press operators occasionally lubricated the die by dipping their hands into a lubricant such as Murphy's Oil Soap and applying it to the die. All that had to be washed off.

It was first washed with soap and alkalies and water softeners and then rinsed. Gray granite ware was made by putting it in a sulphuric acid solution, or sometimes hydrochloric acid. Iron sulphide was added by some manufacturers to the acid because it etched more severely than the others, thereby developing the pattern better. As well as cleaning the shape, the acid solution promoted the adherence of the enamel. Here we are speaking only of ground coats or gray granite ware enamels.

The acid was rinsed off with water and the piece was then neutralized in a soda solution with a little borax in the neutralizing tank. A final hot-water rinse washed off the neutralizer, and the piece was run through a dryer. Then the enamel was applied.

GWII: *The enamel was applied in a different way to obtain gray granite ware than it was to make a white or colored piece, wasn't it?*

Whitehead: Yes. Gray granite ware was made by selective etching. It was dipped in the enamel, dried, and fired. White or colored pieces were made by first applying an enamel ground coat and then a cover coat or finish coat.

In addition to the usual basic ingredients, ground coats contained metallic oxides — usually those of cobalt, nickel, and manganese. These are the

Shaping blanks on a draw press.

65

Worker hand-beading the colored rim on a white dishpan.

elements that became associated with the oxides of iron at the interface between the glass and the steel, thus forming the "bond," which is known as adherence. These elements caused the ground coat to be dark and not particularly attractive, so it was covered by a "cover" coat of almost any desired color.

The subject of adherence has been the crux of literally hundreds of scientific studies and learned dissertations by eminent scholars in the field of ceramics, as well as being the theme of many midnight and later hotel room and barroom discussions. I believe the phenomenon to be both physical and chemical; some fellows believe differently, and some are willing to admit they cannot hold a fixed position on the question.

GWII: *We have read about the cover coat not being acid resistant and another coat being necessary to assure acid resistance. Is this correct?*

Whitehead: You have to be referring to enamels used prior to 1949-1950. Since that time, with the advent of titanium cover coats, everything is acid resistant. In earlier years, those manufacturers who were promoting acid-resisting wares (Polar, Vollrath, some NESCO ware, some Lisk ware, and some U.S.S ware) did use a first coat high in antimony oxide and various flourides, the latter being decidedly non-acid resistant. It was then necessary to add another cover coat with good acid resistance that was inherently less opaque than the first cover coat.

GWII: *We have a labeled Lalance and Grosjean spitcup patented February 13, 1895. It is white with blue trim, but the white looks gray. Was it coated with gray first?*

Whitehead: No. That is how the early white looked. It was difficult to perfect a good pure white. Vollrath strove to make a pure white, and it was his great accomplishment to develop a brilliant white.

GWII: *Can you explain a little more about how gray granite ware was made?*

Whitehead: The dipper picked up a shape such as a dishpan, dipped it into the dip tank, and turned it in a series of deft movements that covered the entire body with enamel. The pattern was developed by a process known as selective etching.

GWII: *What is selective etching?*

Whitehead: It is the way the acid in the enamel oxidizes, or rusts, the steel. The etching was controlled by the type and amount of acid, usually accompanied by sulphates of nickel, copper or, less commonly, cobalt in the enamel. Slow drying time allowed for the etching. The drying time was determined by the humidity and the temperature, and the pattern was developed during the drying process. I'm talking about gray granite ware. Slow drying also prevents cracking or flaking of the bisque.

The best selective etching was achieved by drying progressively at a low temperature with high humidity to a high temperature with low humidity. You see, the steel must rust in order for the pattern to appear.

Canton had the most sophisticated dryer. It was patented by Canton and was developed in conjunction with Carrier, a noted heating, ventilating, and air-conditioning manufacturer. Ware traveled through the dryer just over a third of a mile before entering the furnace. Quite an installation for "country boys!"

GWII: *What is a good example of selective etching?*

Whitehead: The Hoosier pitcher. (Note: See Labels and Trademarks, Columbian.) The dark areas show the rust. The lighter areas show the gray enamel on the areas of the steel that dried before it could rust. You can even see the horizontal lines caused by the action of the spinning lathe when the wrinkles were removed. Each shop performed this in a different way, making its own desired and distinctive patterns.

GWII: *Then all manufacturers made products that had a look unique unto themselves?*

Whitehead: Oh, yes. We in the industry knew the characteristics of each company's wares. We could tell who made it by the feel, weight, style, and texture. All the manufacturers used the same type of processes, but their own designs and color combinations were easily identified by the trade.

GWII: *We understand that gray granite ware is no longer made.*

Whitehead: That's quite true. World War II saw the end of gray granite ware manufacture. Various alphabetized U.S. agencies, through a system of priorities and allocations, placed such stringent limitations on the availability of steel and chemicals, especially cobalt and nickel, that the manufacturers abandoned their lowest-priced lines (including granite ware) through sheer economic necessity.

By the end of the war, hot-rolled steel had been supplanted by the cold-rolling process, the end product of which was not suited for gray granite ware — *sic transit gloria mundi!*

GWII: *After a piece was slowly dried, was it then fired?*

Whitehead: Yes. It was fired in a furnace at a temperature great enough to fuse the glass to the metal. The glass solidified when cooled and remained bonded to the metal.

Electric, oil, or gas-fired box furnaces were first used, but box furnaces were largely supplanted by continuous furnaces starting about 1927. The burning rack held each piece on burning bars so that the entire surface was heated uniformly. Impressions made from the fingerlike projections are often visible on the bottom or under the rims of pans, etc.

GWII: *We have an old gray granite ware mug with four pinpoint marks on the bottom. Were these caused from the pins holding the mug in the furnace?*

Whitehead: Yes. Turn the pieces around and upside-down. You'll see the marks that are not covered with enamel.

GWII: *Then the finished granite ware went to the sorting and wrapping department, as we see in one of the pictures you loaned us?*

Whitehead: There each piece was inspected, labeled, and packed. Bulky pieces, such as ones with handles, were individually wrapped. If they could nest together like pie pans, every other piece was wrapped, thereby saving the expense of labor and materials in the wrapping room. In order to compete, each shortcut had to be utilized.

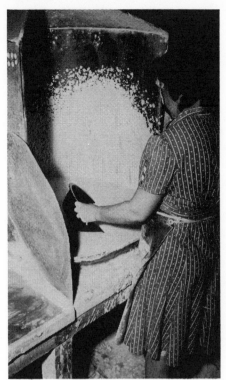

Worker dipping ground-coated dishpan into white enamel.

Worker operating the gas box furnace. Burning points support pans under rims for even heating on burning rack.

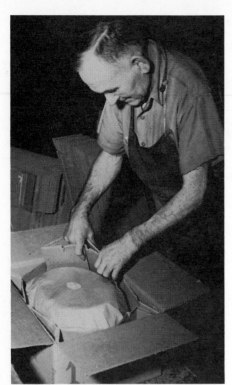

Alternate dishpans are wrapped to conserve paper.

GWII: *How is enamel made?*

Whitehead: Briefly, it is finely ground frit, clay, and water — and color, if desired.

GWII: *What is frit?*

Whitehead: Frit is a partly fused substance used as the basis for enamel. It is made by smelting finely pulverized and mixed materials at high temperatures (2200° to 2500°F.). When this molten mass stops bubbling, it is poured from the smelter into a tank of water and quenched. This produces friable particles known as frit.

Frit was originally used as a verb, meaning to shatter the molten glass into friable particles. The frit is then charged into a ball mill with water and clay and reduced to a fine particle size, and these particles float in the water from the colloidal action of the clay. There are also some chemicals added that affect the mobility and other flow characteristics of the enamel suspension. Color could also be added to the milled enamel. This suspension of the finely divided frit is the enamel that is then used to coat and clean metal base.

GWII: *What is a ball mill?*

Whitehead: It's a large drum where the enamel is made. There are many sizes of mills and balls that are commercially available. We used large ones and small ones. A ball mill six feet in diameter and eight feet long holds about 6,500 pounds of frit. It revolves continuously during one mix time, which is from four to ten hours, and rock balls made of aluminum oxide, mix and grind the frit with the clay and water to produce the enamel. Of course we also used mills so small as to accommodate ten or fifteen pounds of frit.

GWII: *Weren't the rock balls pulverized with all this agitation?*

Whitehead: We used 2½″ to 3″ rock balls in the large mills. They were the hardest rocks man could make. About five pounds of their weight would become part of the frit during one mix time, but that's not much.

GWII: *Do they use ingredients we consider harmful in making frit today?*

Whitehead: No. The ingredients are not harmful.

GWII: *In the late 1800s, customers of a bakery near Boston became ill. Do you think this was caused by the antimony in the enameled kettle that was used to cook the cream filling?*

Sorting and wrapping department, where ware is inspected, labeled, packed, and wrapped.

Whitehead: No. The small amount of antimony in a huge batch of enameling compound was infinitesimal and it had become a part of the molecules of the glaze. Competitors jumped on the opportunity to exploit the illness and made claims of purity and superiority of their product. They used any gimmick to catch a customer's attention.

GWII: *We have always felt that the poisoning was most likely due to salmonella bacilli in the cream filling rather than antimony. Do you agree?*

Whitehead: Yes. The poison claims were never really substantiated, and at that time little was known about germs. Refrigeration was lax or nonexistent. Cream fillings are now accepted as a dangerous medium for growth of germs causing food poisoning.

GWII: *Did you make granite ware for catalog sales?*

Whitehead: Yes. All the companies did. Companies that wanted merchandise for their catalogs put out bid forms specifying quantity, size, color, and even quality (they often bought seconds). We had to sharpen our pencils to get our price low enough to get a big order, yet high enough to make a little profit. We attached labels of their choice right at the plant.

GWII: *Did you make toys?*

Whitehead: We made toys — little teapots, souvenir basins, and buckets. I think all the companies made them at some time, but the bulk of the toys were foreign — mostly German.

GWII: *Did the Depression hurt the granite ware market?*

Whitehead: The Depression actually helped us. We could make and sell it for less than the competition.

GWII: *Did imports hurt?*

Whitehead: Early in the industry, we exported vast amounts of wares. Then it leveled off to equal imports, and later we imported much less than we exported.

We sent our engineers and chemists to underprivileged countries to teach them our techniques, and we created competition. All their cheap labor enabled them to produce ware more cheaply than we could.

GWII: *What are some of the changes and improvements that have been made over the years?*

Emptying a ball mill of a raw enamel batch. Ceramic Coating Company, 1978.

	MALE					FEMALE				
	Start	2 No.	3 No.	Min.	Increase	Start	2 No.	3 No.	Min.	Increase
1937	.45	.50	.55	.60		.35	.38	.42	.45	
1938	.45	.50	.55	.60		.35	.38	.42	.45	
3/1/39	.45	.50	.55	.60		.35	.38	.42	.45	
		4 wk.	4 wk.				4 wk.	4 wk.		
8/18/42	.60	.64	.68	.68	.08	.45	.47	.50½	.50½	.05½
3/13/44	.62	.66	.70	.70	.02	.47	.51	.52½	.52½	.02
6/1/45	.65	.68	.72½	.72½	.02½	.50	.52½	.55	.55	.02½
2/19/46 – Sup.	.83½	.86½	.91	.91	.18½	.68½	.71	.73½	.73½	.18½
9/10/46	.83½	.86½	.91	.91		.68½	.71	.73½	.73½	
5/1/47 – Sup.	.92½	.95½	1.00	1.00	.09	.77½	.80	.82½	.82½	.09
5/1/48 – Sup/	.94½	.97½	1.02	1.02	.02	.79½	.82	.84½	.84½	.02
8/1/48 – Sup.	1.04½	1.07½	1.12	1.12	.10	.87½	.90	.92½	.92½	.08
		20 Days	20 Days				20 Days	20 Days		
1/1/51	1.17½	1.20½	1.25	1.25	.13	1.00½	1.03	1.05½	1.05½	.13
6/4/51	1.20½	1.23½	1.28	1.28	.03	1.03½	1.06	1.08½	1.08½	.03
			Total		.68			Total		.63½
	Percent Increase		113.3			Percent Increase		141.0		

Wage schedule for workers, 1937 to 1951.

Whitehead: The years have seen remarkable improvements in steel quality and enamels and many changes in the methods of preparation, application, and firing of porcelain enameled utensils.

Frit is now made by special manufacturers and sold to the enameling companies. Each enameling company used to make its own frit, but since the frit manufacturers began making it, it was cheaper to buy ready-made frit due to quantity prices, shipping costs, etc. And the quality is excellent. In the late 1950s, Vollrath started buying ready-made frit, and Columbian followed in the early 1960s.

GWII: *Isn't frit made differently, too?*

Whitehead: It was prepared in a batch smelter, but now the greatest tonnage of frit is prepared in continuous smelters. From these, the molten glass issues in a never-ending stream that may be quenched in water or handled on water-cooled stainless alloy rolls. These rolls squeeze the molten glass into ribbons of solid glass, thereby eliminating the need to dry it.

There have also been improvements in enamel frits that enable much thinner coatings to be applied. The thinner the coating, the less tendency for the enamel to chip.

GWII: *You mentioned earlier that the continuous furnace replaced the box furnace. Didn't this reduce labor?*

Whitehead: All "hands-on" operations are costly parts of any process. Ware was conveyed from dip station to dryer, from dryer to furnace, and from furnace to sorting and wrapping with the advent of the continuous furnace. Transfers necessitated by periodic operations were eliminated, and the extra equipment was not needed.

Large baskets were suspended from a trolley on the ceiling. Racks on the baskets held ware, which rested on pins or was suspended on hooks (usually suspended to avoid pin marks).

The trolley, which worked on wheels, carried the baskets from one process to the other continuously.

GWII: *We were told about a "hot dust" or "dry process" of enameling bathtubs by a woman who toured a plant years ago. She remembers seeing a crane lift a big, white-hot bathtub casting from the furnace. A giant sifter coated the bathtub with powdered enamel that looked like powdered sugar, and it melted on contact. Is this still being done?*

Whitehead: For many years, vibrating sieves dusted enamel powder onto a previously heated casting, and the casting was then put back into the furnace and reheated to fuse the enamel uniformly over the surface of cast-iron bathtubs and sinks. This method had a timesaving advantage in that the manufacturer didn't have to wait for the article to cool before applying another coat.

The Koehler Company is still enameling bathtubs by this technique, but by the time of this publication, this could well be a process long gone; the prognosis for cast-iron fixtures is a bit dim.

GWII: *World War II had quite an impact on enameling, didn't it?*

Whitehead: Yes, Although the shortage of critical nickel and heat-resisting alloys during the war ended the production of gray granite ware, it stimulated the development of special types of coatings to resist much higher temperatures and sudden changes in temperatures. After the war, there was a great deal of research for the space program — jet engines, reactors. Heat shields on our shuttle vehicles are prime examples.

GWII: *One last question. Do you use granite ware in your home?*

Whitehead: Absolutely! Always and forever! I've been a "pots and pans" man all my life. It's the most efficient and lasting ware. We (my wife and I) still enjoy cooking with the heavy enameled steel utensils.

One more thing. Let me comment on the Columbian Roaster shown in your Price Guide. That's our Number 300, the last of which was produced in the late 1930s or early 1940's. Note the different mottled pattern on the base and cover, as well as the difference of pattern on the top and sides of the lid.

The cover and base are different because they were made from different sheets of steel, and the double wall of the base caused that piece to dry (thus mottle) differently from the lid. The lid shows two patterns of mottle because in forming the wall, the metal was stretched more than that of the crown, thus altering the grain structure of the metal. This affected the manner in which the acid attacked the metal in pickling, as well as the growth of the iron oxide (rust) crystals during the drying (mottling) process.

GWII: *We can't thank you enough! You have made a complicated subject much more comprehensible.*

Worker unloading a smelt of frit, which is being water-quenched. The Ceramic Coating Company, Newport, Kentucky, 1978.

How It Was Assembled

Spouts. Since granite ware manufacturers made their own parts, the methods of designing and attaching the parts were developed by trial and error. Early spouts were riveted, soldered or welded. The Niedringhaus patent illustrated the way tabs were inserted into slots, bent over, and enameled to secure their placement.

These spouts often leaked, and unhappy customers returned the defective pots for refunds or replacements. Later, when the spouts were stamped out with the bodies from one piece of steel, this problem was solved.

Welding was an improvement and became an important part of the industry. Welded parts had a strong, clean union and, when the ware was enameled, there was no sign of rivets or solder. Spouts were applied to individual pieces by hand. The welder made about thirty cents an hour, and the coffeepots sold for twenty cents, wholesale.

Teapot spouts were placed near the base of the pots. Coffeepot spouts were attached at the top of the pots. Coffee grounds stayed at the bottom of the pots, and any residue was filtered out. Coffee biggins, however, had teapot spouts, probably to prevent overflow. It was easy to pour more water than was needed into the top section of the biggins. The grounds were contained in the basket rather than the bottom of the pots.

Handles. The most important parts of granite ware were the handles. If they were not sturdy, cooks could be injured, food spilled and wasted, or children burned. At the very least, a faulty handle caused a great deal of frustration.

Syrup pitcher with welded spout and spout cover that have been added to a coffeepot body. There is no strainer in the spout.

Left: Strap handle welded with rivets. Iron handles were used on lids through the 1920s. Simple wire handle was slipped through a channel and welded from inside the lid.

There were many attempts at designing practical handles. One of the best was for the threaded spoon handle. This spoon was stamped in one piece and then crimped to form a groove that ran the length of the handle and into the bowl. This created a strong spoon handle with a pleasing design. The spoon handle joined by a rivet at the bowl was inferior to the threaded spoon handle.

Some of the first handles were made of iron, in one piece. They are harder to find today because they were weaker than the two-piece iron handles that replaced them. An early Granite Iron Ware cookbook advertised one-piece iron handles on Imperial coffeepots, teapots, milk pitchers, and water carriers. The handles were attached to the bodies by long rivets placed at the double seam to provide added strength. The rivets were capped with knobs that made the handles project quite a distance from the bodies.

The St. Louis Stamping Company applied two-piece iron handles to their one-cup teapots at an early date. These pots bore the company's earliest trademark. Identical handles were attached to Iron Clad coffeepots and molasses pitchers, as well as Lalance and Grosjean's Agate Iron Ware coffeepots, dated "Pat. Oct. 1889," while different iron handles were used on Lalance and Grosjean milk pitchers and Windsor teapots. Later, iron handles were made in which the two pieces were part of the design. All iron handles were painted black. Most found today have traces of paint.

Wooden-handled pieces are hard to find because, although they were less likely to burn the cook's hands, they were more likely to be damaged by the heat from the stove. Teakettles or coffee boilers that once had wooden grips may be identified by the shape of the bails. Curved bails never had wooden grips.

Water often damaged long, wooden dipper handles, but the short, heavy handles on flat-bottom dippers were stronger. Short-handled dippers were used for dipping suds in breweries, feeding grain to horses, scooping peanuts in the general store, and even for serving large portions of stew to hungry harvesters.

Wire bail handles were common on coffee boilers, water carriers, preserve kettles, teakettles, milk kettles, cream cans, combinets, and slop jars. They were attached by loops of wire, which ran around and under the rim, or by other types of ears.

Wire threaded through the rim of this bucket forms an ear loop for the wire handle.

Handle on milk kettle and tin lid, riveted and welded.

Children often carried their school lunches in small buckets. Evelyn Welch once held up a tiny, covered bailed kettle when she presented a program on granite ware and said, "This was sold to me as a lunch bucket, but I think it's too small."

An elderly lady spoke up, "When I started to school in Nebraska, buckets like that sold for ten cents. I wanted one so badly, but by the time I had saved a dime, I had grown enough to need a larger bucket for my lunch!"

Bailed buckets were also used for berry picking. Collectors refer to berry buckets, but we have never found this listing in any research material. Bail handles were not successful and few are made today.

Large coffeepots and boilers had strap handles on their sides to help tip them safely. Single pieces of metal were riveted before being enameled, and some of these strap handles were thin and did not support the weight of the vessels.

Western movie fans may conjure up the familiar picture of the roundup campfire, in which the cook whisked his red bandana from his back pocket and used the bandana as a potholder to grasp the strap handle on a gray granite coffee boiler.

In 1928, Vollrath advertised smooth, rounded handles with completely rolled-under sides that left no sharp, jagged edges to hurt the hands. "The handles cannot possibly come off, loosen, or leak at the joint, because the joint between the handle and the bowl is fused and it is stronger than even the steel in the vessel itself. Hollow handles such as Vollrath advertised were superior to other handles. They were stronger, safer, and easier to use.

Knobs. Similar to handles in design and material, knobs shared some of the problems of handles, too. Wooden knobs burned; iron knobs loosened, and wire and strap knobs weakened.

Iron knobs were among the first to be used by the St. Louis Stamping Company and Iron Clad Manufacturing Company. Wire and thin metal strap knobs were useful as a means of getting a good grip on tight-fitting lids on milk cans. And the hollow-type Crown Cover Knobs, named for their appearance, proved best until glass and porcelain entered the competition.

Ears. No other parts reflected the individuality of the manufacturers more than the ears. Each design and application projected its own personality.

Potmakers and tinsmiths used the term "ears" to describe the pierced metal plates, riveted or soldered on either side of the rims to which the handles were attached.

There were other kinds of ears, too. Some were stamped into the form and some were made from the continuous wire that rimmed the bead. A few handles were simply lapped over the edge of the rim and riveted onto the side of the vessels.

Hooks riveted and welded to "Handihook Lids, Republic Metalware Company, Patent Dec 17, 1912."

The method of applying these iron handles is described in one of Niedringhaus' patents. Handle on left is loose, which is probably the reason few survived.

Notches on ears of kettles lock bails in position, thereby protecting the wooden handles. No danger to "Alaska" wire spiral handle. Note its beautiful pattern.

1920s double boiler insert has hollow handle and wooden knob on tin lid. Catalogs filled orders with tin lids unless otherwise specified. Enameled lids were an additional one dollar per dozen.

Dipper handles were nailed to an enameled ferrule, which was riveted and welded to the cup.

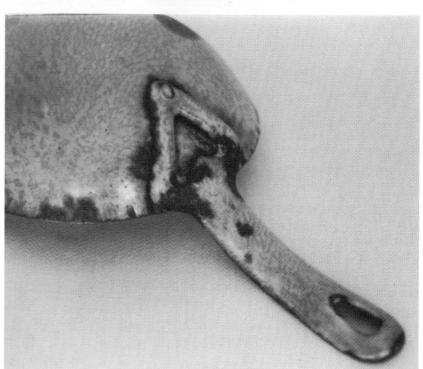

Handle riveted and welded directly on scoop.

Handle secured by rivets, welded, and nailed cap.

Manufacturers designed and made their own parts. These diverse ears reflect the makers' individuality.

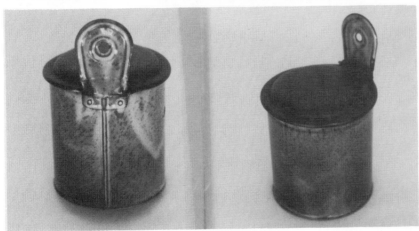

Early Haberman Brothers round salt box has seamed bottom and body and a tin lid. The pierced hanging tab was riveted and welded to withstand weight of the salt.

Notched ear enables the bail to be locked in place.

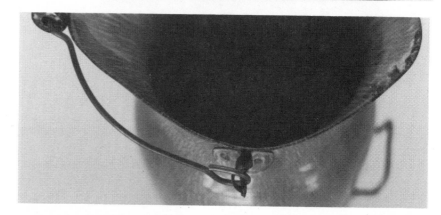

How It Was Decorated

Women were encouraged to modernize their kitchens. NESCO urged women to enjoy cooking by equipping their kitchens with the oil cookstove and their Royal Enameled Ware.

In typically understated British tone, *The English Cyclopaedia* of 1867, quoted here, predicted the blossom before the apple: And in sixty years, under proper direction, color in the kitchen became "one of the most important and significant housewares merchandising developments in the United States," according to Earl Lifshey.

Most of the early granite ware was gray. It could be made in one step, so it was cheaper and quicker to make than colored ware, which needed at least two coats. Still, beautifully colored enamelware was made early on. A delicate turquoise or robin's-egg blue ware called Niagara was pictured in the 1909 *Republic Metalware Company Catalog.*

It wasn't until after World War I, wrote Howard Ketcham in *The Enamelist*, that women became eager to brighten and cheer up their kitchens. At that time, industries began catering to homemakers' desire for colored home kitchen equipment. One manufacturer introduced a refrigerator entirely in color.

Home magazine editors and writers, interior decorators, and retailers suggested new ways for the housewife to decorate with color. As a result, in six months' time, the sales of colored kitchen stoves and refrigerators rose from 30 percent to 70 percent.

Ketcham thought that this could be a trend and that future sales of housewares could be controlled and stimulated by the popularity of certain colors. He was right. Over the years, we have seen color fad cycles of pink, yellow, aqua, avocado, harvest gold, and copper. Now we have swung back to sanitary white, gray, black, almond, and Delft blue. Ketcham was a pioneer in testing consumer color preferences and in developing and standardizing colors for industrial groups and manufacturers.

By 1928, colored enameled cookware was on its way to becoming the major sales promotion over other competitive metal finishes, according to Lifshey. This was the time when Henry Ford offered to sell his customers a Model T "in any color they want — as long as it's black." And it was years before color was introduced in home furnishings.

Macy's president, Jesse I. Straus, had seen some colored enamelware in Paris. He told his buyer, Joseph P. Kasper, about a white cereal set that had a flamelike design of red streaks outlined in gold. Kasper found the set in Paris and brought back a sample. He took it to Vollrath's Vice-President of Sales, DeWitt Reese, and within a month's time, Reese had developed samples to show to Kasper.

Lifshey describes Joe Kasper's enthusiasm, "What a sight! They had made up a one-quart saucepan for every college color combination in the country and arranged them all on shelves in their big sample room. They had black and orange for Princeton . . . . You name it and they had it. There was gray inside, red outside — and then it was reversed. It was really terrific!"

The porcelain enamel industry was highly creative and competitive. Besides the vast range of solid colors, enamelware was decorated in a

---

Enamelled Ware

Plates, dishes, &c., produced by this process for table use are susceptible of any amount of decoration, in the manner and the methods applicable to ordinary earthenware or porcelain, and are peculiarly suitable for ship purposes from their lightness and non-liability to fracture. In many decorative purposes this method of enamelling on sheet iron is likely, under proper direction, to become of great value and importance.

— The English Cyclopaedia, 1867

Flow-Coating a Casserole, by Merlin H. Whitehead: "At point (1) is a fountain, which delivered fluid enamel to the interior of the ware when the operator placed it over the activating yoke (2) and depressed the yoke. The operator then positioned the casserole over the end of the work-holder, which is in its closed position.

Now look at point (7) and see the work-holder in its open position. The closing was accomplished by means of a shoe being forced against the end of the work-holder by an air cylinder, thrusting it toward the operator and collapsing the three toggles, thus reducing the diameter of the outer ends of the holder to accept the ware placed thereon (3). Sorry you can't see this; the mechanism is back there in the dark under all the supporting framework.

Next the ware was elevated and rotated about 45 degrees (4) to drain and smooth the enamel. The machine operated with a load-bearing chain traveling from operators left to right. Then the holder was depressed to about 22 degrees above horizontal and, as it passed under the flow-coater (5), a little flap opened about ¹⁄₁₆″, allowing a sheet of enamel to flow over the continuously rotating piece. The flow-coater applied either the same color as the fountain, or a different color.

Ware then entered an enclosed chamber (again not in our view, being 'downstream' behind the flow-coater) where it was exposed to rather gentle drafts of warm air to assure that the enamel was rendered immobile once the desired coating had been obtained.

At point (6), the ware emerged from the chamber to rotate against a counter-rotating wheel, covered 'tire-fashion' with indoor-outdoor carpeting material, to remove the enamel from the rim in order that the stainless steel band could be applied without cracking the enamel and also so that the band would fit properly.

Ware proceeded to the unloading station, opposite the loading station, where another operator, using special tools designed to handle the ware without making marks, transferred the ware to the furnace chain, which carried it through the dryer and furnace. Until it was dry, it could not be touched, for it was still mushy and easily ruined.

At point (7), the work-holder is shown in the open position, having just left the brushing station, where it passed over a rapidly rotating brush with long, tough, yet pliable synthetic bristles that removed the enamel from the gripping needles at the ends of the holder arms. This was the end of the cycle of this forty-foot machine. The cycle was repeated to produce four to five thousand pieces per eight-hour shift, which translated to about one hundred sixty full cycles per shift."

variety of textures and prints. Colored enamel was made by adding metallic oxides to the frit: lead or antimony for yellow; gold or iron for red; and copper, cobalt, or iron for green. Violets and a great variety of intermediate colors were produced by mixing the oxides in different proportions.

Enamel was applied by hand dipping, machine dipping, tong dipping, pouring, and spraying — techniques that are illustrated by photographs in this section and also in the "Illustrated Price Guide."

Dippers became highly skilled at turning and draining a piece for a look they desired — the bark on a tree, glacial striae, or the foam on ocean waves. These effects were achieved by years of experience.

Dippers also used tongs to grip a piece without causing streaks. The operator dipped the ware into the enamel and drained off the excess to achieve a smooth finish. The consistency of the enamel was important. It had to flow smoothly on the piece and still have enough body to hold itself in place.

This was also an important consideration in spraying the enamel. In addition, the spray had to be dry enough to prevent roughening by the air from the gun. E. E. Bryant wrote in *The Enamelist* that the spray gun had to be properly adjusted so that the angle of the drain would be correct. The final finish of the enamel was largely dependent upon the quality of the application. Raw shapes had to be free of dents and imperfections, or else chipping resulted.

After the solid color, or white, was applied, the hollowware could be decorated by means of the following techniques:

Automatic highlighting. As an enameled piece rotated on a mechanical axis, an air-operated gun sprayed it with a lighter or darker shade of enamel to highlight the surface.

Beading. This was also known as rimming. One operator wiped off the wet slip on the rim of a shape and passed it to another worker, who applied the decorative color by hand. Beading also was done mechanically. A fabric-covered wheel removed the wet enamel from the rim as another applied the colored bead.

Brushing. Decorations were applied by daubing them with a paint brush. To obtain a natural wood-grained effect, a graining paste was brushed on an enameled surface.

Machine dip-draining. Roasters and covers were submerged in a vat of enamel to produce the single-coat black with white-speck enamelware.

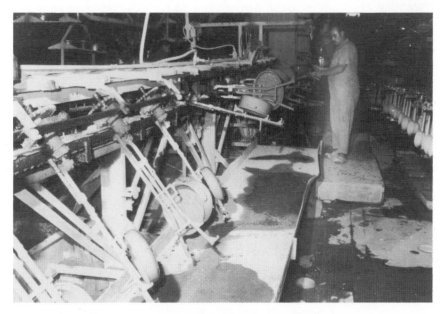

Pieces were then drained at carefully determined altitudes for carefully determined times. This unit produced up to twelve hundred pieces per hour.

Saucepans were enameled with a cover coat. Tools were designed to accommodate three sizes without a change of setting. This provided a convenient mix of sizes according to production requirements, which could easily be packed into nested sets. Sixteen hundred pieces produced per hour.

Machine flow-coating. This machine coated outside with one color, inside with another.

In the same cycle, the bead was wiped and the ware trimmed with a third color. Six hundred fifty pieces were produced per hour.

Automatic highlighting. Spray gun and turntable were electrically timed to synchronize so that the turntable started before the gun and stopped after the gun. It produced six hundred pieces per hour.

Applying decals — decalcomania. Decals were purchased from ceramic decal supply houses. They were printed with ceramic colors, and their paper backings were coated with flux — a substance used to promote the fusion of the metal. The flux melted at a lower temperature than the rest of the enamel. If the design sank into the enamel, "it was usually cause for complaint," remarked Whitehead, "and the manufacturer was asked to harden the flux a bit."

The decals were loosened from their paper backings in water and slipped onto a fired surface. When the piece was fired again, the decals became an integral part of the coating.

Decals were applied to Fiesta, Federal's Rose, and Lisk-Savory's Clam Steamers, as well as to Vollrath's Provincial and Town and Terrace designs. Blue Onion and Willow Ware patterns were also decorated by decals. These patterns were initiated by Whitehead when he was at Columbian.

Vollrath ads stated that designs were permanently fired into their glowing, gleaming, white porcelain on steel, and that the designs would not wash or wear off.

Sometimes even trademarks were fired on decals. Victorian floral and scenic decals were applied to Manning-Bowman's "Patent Decorated Pearl Agateware," which was advertised in the catalog as being beautifully decorated by hand. Apparently this meant that the decals were put on by hand.

It is obvious that there was considerable difference in the amount of flux used on many designs. The Indian portrait decals on the plate and tumbler shown in this book had little flux, while a good deal more was used on the apple, grape, and strawberry motifs on Corona ware and on the incised figures of animals and children on the plates and potties shown. The flux on the latter pieces makes up part of the design.

Embossing. By this process, the decorations were die-stamped into the shapes. Highlights and shadows appeared when the pieces were enameled. Embossing was described in *The English Cyclopaedia*, 1867:

> We may advert in this place, as belonging quite as much to the enamelling art as to that of earthenware or porcelain, to the Baron De Tremblay's émail ombrant, or *shaded enamel* — a production remarkable alike for the ingenious way in which it is wrought and for the pleasing appearance which it is said to present. It consists in flooding coloured but transparent glazes over designs stamped in the body of earthenware. A plain surface is thus produced, in which the cavities of the stamped design appear as shadows of various depths, the parts in highest relief coming nearest the surface of the glaze, and thus leaving the effect of lights of the picture.

Beading. With a predetermined sequence of motions, one operator dipped the ware into the enamel (tong dipping), another wiped the bead, and a third worker manually applied the decorative beading and transferred the item to the burning chain. This team produced two hundred fifty to nine hundred pieces per hour. This was the most common method of applying enamel in 1935.

Decalcomania. Worker applied decals.
The work holder was composed of a ball
bearing mounted shaft with three slots,
which received three tiered segments secured by a stout elastic band.

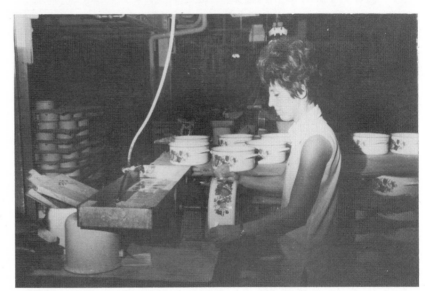

Workers could apply decals to one hundred thirty-five to two hundred twenty
pieces per hour.

Decals. Holly Hobbie, 1937 King George
VI and Queen Elizabeth.

Decals. Lisk-Savory's Fiesta and Vollrath's Town & Terrace.

Federal's Rose, Columbian's Blue Willow, and Savory's Clam Steamers.

Vollrath's Provincial Ware and Dutch Tulip by Prizer-Ware.

Decal on diaper pail.

Turkey platter made in the Orient. Note the considerable amount of flux used on these decals.

Examples of the wonderful effects of selective etching.

One of the most sought after pieces of all granite ware is the children's ABC plate with embossed lettering.

Hand painting. Hand-painted enamelware advertisements, we believe, were misleading. Manning-Bowman advertised that their granite ware was hand painted, and they claimed that noted American artists painted their designs.

An 1885 *Horton, Gilmore, McWilliams and Company Wholesale Catalog* advertised Manning-Bowman coffeepots and teapots as "Pearl Agate Ware. Patent Decorated, Hand Painted in Mineral Colors." An old Manning-Bowman catalog shows a "Patent Decorated Pearl Agateware Sleeping and Parlor Car Spittoon," captioned, "Two sides of the same article, one with name and the other with floral decoration, both hand-painted."

Whitehead states, "I do not know of any hand-painted enamelware. It was much too costly to produce."

Most likely, hand painting meant that the original designs were hand painted by artists, then reproduced on decals that were applied by hand. The paintings are identical. Such preciseness would have been impossible, considering that thousands and thousands were made.

Precipitating salts. Application and effect were described in a paper presented at the Fiftieth Annual Meeting of The American Ceramic Society, Chicago, April, 1948, by George Sirovy and Edmund P. Czolgos.

> The marble-like finish so developed consists of deep-colored veins, approximately $\frac{1}{32}$ in. thick, entwining and enclosing irregular-shaped, interjoined, lighter-colored mottles having very light centers, ranging in size up to approximately 1½ sq. in."

This design was achieved by applying enamel slip over a half-finished, fired white base. While still moist, crystals of precipitating salts were scattered uniformly about one inch apart on the enamel. Mottling developed as the precipitating salts dissolved in the moist enamel and reacted with the incorporated mottling salts.

When dried and fired, the surface had the appearance of marble. This method is similar to one used by Europeans to produce a marbled finish. They sprinkled enamel slips on a fired ground coat. Then, while the slips were still moist, they dusted the surface with crystals of soda or pearl ash. The marble developed when fired.

Sirovy and Czolgos reported that mottles were developed in ivory, yellow, red, burgundy, blue, lavender, green, and brown.

Printing. Marbling, graining, and repeated designs were printed on an enameled surface by either of two methods: Rolling a roll with a design onto a color oxide oil paste and then onto the enameled surface, or rolling a smooth roll onto a printed slab, thereby picking up the inked design and transferring it to the enameled piece. Table tops were textured in this way.

Selective etching. This is the method used to develop the pattern on gray granite ware. It was described in detail by Whitehead in our interview. He stated that the pattern developed by selective etching is called mottling.

Mottling has a number of meanings. The American Ceramic Society, in its 1949 Glossary, defined it as "A finish, usually gray, composed of a series of spots of various depths of color, reproducing in enamel the appearance of coarse granite structure."

Sirovy and Czolgos, in their 1949 paper, stated that the mottled one-coat ware produced by kitchenware manufacturers was made by selective etching. They also wrote about the colored mottle finishes developed by the precipitating salts method.

To add to the confusion, a variety of colored ware was advertised as mottled. In 1910, the Biddle Hardware Company advertised Columbia's "Onyx Ware" as rich brown and heavily mottled with white. To collectors, mottled means the marble pattern resulting from splash stippling.

Stamped "Granite SECONDS." Lifshey told of stores long gone and once famous, like Hearns on New York's Fourteenth Street and the Fair Store on Chicago's State Street, which would periodically run enormous floor-wide promotions on speckled gray enamelware, often featuring seconds. "Indeed, it got to be something of a standing joke that the factories would 'make seconds to order' for those sales."

Silk screening. This was a method of printing a colored design through the threads of silk or a fabric in which some areas had been blocked to resist the enamel.

Columbian's Frontier Ware, initiated by Whitehead, was decorated by silk screening. The white letters on the Stransky & Co. tray were silk screened, too. After the ground coat and the two blue coats were fired on this tray, the background was blocked out, leaving the lettered areas to be squeegeed with white enamel. It was then fired a final time.

Speckling. Lisk-Savory Imperial Blue Enameled Ware and the contemporary dark blue speckled ware (available in many stores) are both good examples of speckling.

In Whitehead's collection of photographs of Canton Stamping, a worker demonstrated how the specks of enamel were spattered on by the brush. They could also be spattered by hand.

Flecks are now produced by the addition of sized particles of frit of a different color. White is added to the blue mixture in the ball mill about five minutes before the end of the grind.

Splash stippling. This was another method of obtaining a marbleized or mottled effect. Various colored enamels were splashed on a cover coat by a worker who shook the piece and allowed the enamel to drain at various angles. Collectors commonly call this mottling.

Stamping. "Seconds" were stamped with ceramic ink, which was composed of ceramic oxide suspended in a suitable oil vehicle. Sometimes trademarks also were stamped on.

Stenciling. A stencil is a thin brass plate or a piece of heavily waxed cardboard from which a design is cut. Colored enamel was brushed on or rolled over the stencil, then the piece was fired. The Polar Ware ashtray was stenciled. On a large area such as a tabletop, the enamel may be sprayed over the stencil with an airbrush.

The ultimate in decorating was achieved on the elaborate Royal Granite Steel Ware tray. "Probably only a few of these trays were made," said Whitehead. "They were most likely commemorative pieces. This one has a heavy enameled surface which was very expensive to make."

Whitehead explained the steps involved in creating this tray. "First it was enameled in gray, and the pattern was formed by selective etching. The dark blue with white was then brushed on the border. The lettering and center design were blocked out by silk screening. Then, while the dark blue and white border was still somewhat moist, the entire tray was coated with the light blue. The addition of extra clay in the light blue enamel produced a chemical reaction which made the enamel shrink, yet cover and flow into the dark blue border, creating a coarse marbled effect."

Stenciling on Polar Ware ashtray. Decals on other pieces.

This design and similar designs were printed on table tops.

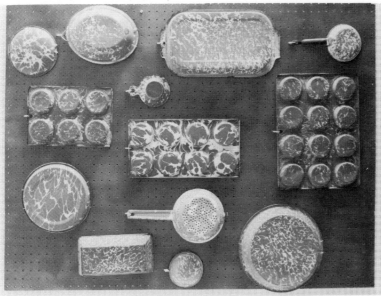

Splash stippling, popularly known as mottling.

Columbian's Frontier Ware, decorated by silk screening.

Care and Repair

Repairing granite ware was an economic necessity at one time. In those days, it was routine for farmers to repair leaking water buckets or pans with copper rivets at the same time they were mending their harnesses and saddles.

Commercial products were also available. Mendets were similar to copper rivets, and So-luminum was a plastic recommended for mending metals and enameled wares. For authentic and aesthetic reasons, collectors still use Mendets to patch holes.

Methods of caring for and cleaning granite ware appeared in cookbooks as early as 1924. *The Home Comfort Range Cook Book* recommended softening lime deposits on teakettles by boiling a few stalks of rhubarb. Burned or discolored ware could be cleaned with salt and vinegar and, grease could be removed with a cloth saturated in kerosene. Tea and coffee stains would disappear by boiling a teaspoon of soda in the kettle or pot for three-quarters of an hour! A cookbook in 1925 advised airing out teapots and coffeepots to prevent mustiness.

These are still effective means of cleaning granite ware, and there are a number of new products on the market. Salt and vinegar will sweeten and clean most enameled surfaces, and an overnight soaking in a baking soda solution will loosen burned-on food. Kerosene is excellent for removing the rust on canister and flask lids, and it does not damage the enamel. Household bleach will remove most stains, and Lime A-Way Bathroom Cleaner® will quickly dissolve mineral deposits in teakettles and double boilers.

The old and the new can be maintained in bright purity. The old enamelware never had enough poison in its coating to be dangerous, and present government regulations would forbid new enamelware on the market if it were not safe. Use it and enjoy it.

Mended pie pan. Note cracks made by repairing. "So-Luminum, for Pans, Wood, Glass, Porcelain — All Metals." "Mendets." The six Mendets cards that are known may be easily dated by hairstyles and clothing on the women pictured in the ads.

Decorating with Granite Ware

Granite ware in Elaine and Larry Erwin's bathroom blends beautifully with old shaving accessories.

Elaine Erwin's cozy kitchen corner has red-and-white wallpaper that gives gray granite ware a colorful place to stake its claim.

Brenda Hutto is the wife of a military medical officer. She filled her old store cabinet and a wall shelf with blue-and-white mottled enamelware to achieve that old home feeling with every move.

Evelyn Welch's clock was made from a gray frying pan and a battery kit. It fits into country decor in any area in the house.

Elizabeth and Robert Cole are the fifth generation to live in the oldest house in their city. The house was built in 1868, and Elizabeth has decorated it with antiques. Note enameled cast-iron pancake griddle at top, center. Pictured in iron in the Sears, Roebuck and Company catalog, 1897, it is advertised as heating quickly. "The batter is poured into the little round hinged pans. When done on the first side, the round pans are turned over with a fork into the long pan. While they are cooking the round pans are refilled."

What Happened to Granite Ware

In 1945, there were seventeen companies in the United States making granite ware. Today there is one.

At one time, the granite ware industry was prosperous. Its craftsmen learned to enamel steel as well as iron. They developed continuous furnaces, discovered high-speed ground coats, and learned how to apply enamels directly to steel. But in spite of the growth and progress, the industry plummeted.

Fredrick Petersen explained, "Industry sales decreased, we believe, because of competition from imported products, changes in other types of utensils, and the introduction of plastic utensils such as pails, basins, etc." In 1958, the Enameled Utensils Manufacturing Council disbanded due to the decline of the industry.

"Aluminum really hurt granite ware in the 1920s, and then Pyrex®, Corning Ware®, and stainless steel took their toll," says Merlin Whitehead. "The rising costs of materials and labor, plus increased taxes, also affected production. But we must not overlook the economic evolution in America. When many housewives were employed during World War II, they could afford prepared foods for their families. This stimulated a market for canned, dried, and frozen foods. The roasters and canners that kept the business alive during the Depression and the war years were no longer able to sustain the industry."

Gradually, the manufacturers either closed for financial reasons, sold out or merged, or converted to making plastic or steel products. In 1968, only Columbian and the United States Stamping Company remained. Columbian was sold to General Housewares Corporation in 1968, and the United States Stamping Company closed before the plant burned in 1982.

By 1978, nearly 35 percent of enameled cookware came to the United States from Mexico, Taiwan, and South Korea. To protect General Housewares from the rising number of foreign imports, President Jimmy Carter approved an International Trade Commission's recommendation to impose additional duties on enamelware imports. When the expiration date for this tariff neared, General Housewares requested an extension, which they later withdrew when attorneys for the foreign companies opposed it.

General Housewares was then instrumental in removing their major competitors in Taiwan from the duty-free General Systems of Preferences. A new tariff was imposed on enamelware from Taiwan. This made American prices competitive with Taiwan's.

The struggle continues, however. Microwave ovens have had an adverse affect on the market, and foreign manufacturers have long felt the impact of the changes in the American life-styles.

There are still opportunities for collectors, though, so take heart. Housewares departments are displaying fine new utensils of porcelain enamel, which are handsomely decorated and well constructed. They will be the next century's antiques. Also, there still are mysteries in granite ware's history that collectors will be challenged to solve. But, best of all, there are still rare pieces to find.

Row 1: Teakettle, 3½", blue, rare. **$125**
Blue mottled teakettle, rare. **$125**
Row 2: White tumbler with cobalt and gold trim. **$38**
Row 3: Mug, blue, 2". **$35**
Blue salt box, wooden lid, 3½", rare. **$125**
Blue mug, 1½". **$38**
Row 4: Chamber pot, blue and white, 2¼". **$75**

Illustrated Price Guide

Toys and Children's Items

French catalogs listed Enameled Toy Household Sets *(Ménages én fer Émaille)* as early as 1884, and there were other early foreign made toys. Some of them were sold by Marshall Field. In that company's 1914 catalog a blue tea set with "Bulgarian" decorations in white, red, and yellow was offered.

We do not know how many other of the advertised sets were foreign made, however. Fields also listed a sixteen-piece set in blue decorated with white squares; a sixteen-piece set in white with pink roses; an expensive gray set in gray shaded to white with roses and gold rims; and a white set decorated with a navy blue chain pattern and gold rims. These tea sets often included teaspoons of heavy tin or nickel.

Thanks to two collectors in Ohio and Pennsylvania, we are privileged to show some particularly rare toys, such as teakettles, mixing spoons, spice racks, utensil racks, a wall rack with cup hooks, soap dishes, salt boxes, and candleholders.

Alphabet plates like the gray ABC plate pictured were shown in a *Granite Iron Ware Cookbook* in the 1880s. Lalance and Grosjean also made them. Toy plates are popular items. A 1940s Mickey Mouse plate marked "England" recently sold for $45.

Sand play set, early 1900s, lavender. **$175**

Toy stove, 7"x11"x5". Original pit bottom utensils fit down into the eyes of the stove. Note water heater with faucet and brass flue fitting. **$1,100**

Gray tea set with eight-ounce teapot and six cups and saucers. **$300**

White dinner set with gold grapeleaf trim. Has nine soup plates, tureen with lid and ladle, gravy boat, platter, and divided vegetable dish. **$350**

Partial toy set. Blue, green, burgundy, and navy spatter on white frying pan, soap dish, platter, sauce kettle, and mixing bowls. **$175**

Diaper pail, white with blue. **$35**

Wash set. Soap dish, sponge dish, bowl, pitcher, and bucket in green with white speckles. **$150**

Blue-and-white cuspidor. **$85**
Spice rack with containers. **$150**
Utensil rack, ladle, and strainer. **$150**
Wall rack for soap with original cup. **$125**
Candlestick. **$100**
Blue-and-white potty. **$75**

Sterno vaporizer or bottle warmer. **$38**

Green Chrysolite child's mug. **$32**
Mug. **$12**
Green mug, cream lining, "Vollrath, U.S.A." **$20**

Colander, 3¾″x1⅞″. Mint. **$85**
Cake pan, ¾″x4″. **$35**
Preserve kettle, domestic science, 1⅝″x4″. **$35**

Advertising

Fairs and expositions provided the first means of advertising granite ware. City and country people swarmed to these festive events. Manufacturers displayed their newest products and competed for prizes. Grand Gold Medals were presented to Agate Iron Ware at the 1878 Paris Exhibition and in New Orleans in 1884-1885.

The Iron Clad Manufacturing Company gave away postcards and booklets at the Columbian Exposition in Chicago in 1893 and ashtrays at the Pan American Exposition in Buffalo, New York, 1901.

The National Enameling and Stamping Company dedicated a dainty little "Pot Luck" booklet to "the fair sex of Glorious America," at the St. Louis Exposition. The booklet had an early NESCO label, indicated by the same gray kettle used by the St. Louis Stamping Company, and for a time, after 1899, when it became NESCO. Two NESCO factories were pictured and described as the largest and most complete in the world, and Royal Granite Steel Ware was said to be "the great purchase today," although the Louisiana Purchase "is unequaled in the history of the world."

Stickpins, watchfobs, measures, match holders, and pocket knives were also given to visitors at the factories and home offices. Thatcher Ranges, Boilers, and Furnaces gave enameled cast iron paperweights inscribed, "Your Warm Friend."

Manufacturers also gave trade cards with their names or trademarks printed on the front and the dealer's name on the back. The St. Louis Stamping Company lithographed high quality cards of children using granite ware. Some of their cards were printed with French captions for the large French population of St. Louis or for foreign distribution.

There were trade cards that depicted political satire. But some of the most popular trade cards were enlarged and offered for fifteen cents postage. "Gran-ie-ta" and "Granite Ironware Is All The Gossip" were made into cloth-backed enlargements. They are rare and highly prized by contemporary collectors. They also are highly priced. The "Granite Ironware Is All The Gossip" card is the only copy known to exist, and the owners display it in their home as a lovely art treasure. It is shown in the Color Section.

"Patent Granite Iron Ware" trade card. Color. **$15**

"Patent Granite Iron Ware" trade card. Color. **$15**

Page from Geuder, Paesche & Frey Company Catalog showing advertising display.

98

There were many fine advertising artists. The colors are still vivid on the Geuder, Paeschke, and Frey Company "Tulip Ware" store sign. The design is artistically pleasing. The life-size NESCO-lady store display, in the Color Section, is so realistic that a visitor in the owner's home was startled when she confronted the cardboard figure in the dark. The "Old Dutch Cleanser" and "Lifesavers" enameled signs are also attractive art works.

One of the first advertising dates appears on a St. Louis Stamping Company cookbook. This June 1874, cookbook contained recipes and advice for women on how to prepare nutritious meals, brew outstanding coffee, entertain properly, and utilize every cut of meat. This gives us insight into the American homemaker of the day. It reveals her interests, her values, and her life-style. In *Understanding Media*, 1964, Marshall McLuhan wrote: "The historians and archeologists will one day discover that the ads of our times are the richest and most faithful daily reflections that any society ever made of its entire range of activities."

Magazine ads provide us with various clues that tell us women were concerned with all aspects of their families' welfare. They wanted their families to be healthy, happy, and prosperous. Magazine ads told them how. Lalance and Grosjean advertised in the April, 1901, *McClure's Magazine:*

> Buy kitchen utensils as you'd gather mushrooms. Insure yourself against poison. You turn over a mushroom and look at the pink gills. You turn over a piece of enameled ware to look for this trademark. "Agate Nickel-Steel Ware" is SAFE. Send for our booklet showing why only "Agate Nickel-Steel Ware" is safe and why either Arsenic, Antimony or Lead is found in the goods of the *seventeen* other manufacturers of enameled ware!

A NESCO ad in the August, 1923, *Modern Priscilla Magazine* stated:

> Granite ware for canning reminds one of childhood days and the joys of happy anticipation over Grandmother's fruits and preserves, as they used to simmer in her blue-gray granite kettle. Now, as in Grandmother's time, acid fruits or mineral-rich vegetables for canning and preserving are safe when cooked in "Royal Granite Enameled Ware."

In the November, 1921, *Ladies' Home Journal*, Vollrath stressed the sanitary appeal of the pure, white ware that would not harbor dirt, grime, or germs. Many other companies claimed that their products were pure, and some hired chemists to test for poisons. Testimonials of the findings of these scientists were then printed in magazine ads and on labels. Happiness was related to color, according to Vollrath's ad in the October, 1930, *Good Housekeeping:*

> Vollrath color ware gives charm and cheer. Its gayety of color will have a daily influence on your happiness. It's easy on your hands, your time and your temper.

Vollrath advertised that their brilliant hues and pleasing pastel tints — Delft Blue, Mandarin Red, Apple Green, and Old Rose — were the latest in kitchen beauty. Savory suggested standardizing Savory Ware to make "your kitchen a happier and more convenient workshop!"

An Enterprise Enamel Company early ad emphasized that their Corona ware was the only decorated enamelware made, that it came in many beautiful colors, and that it was "made attractive by a famous American artist." To be more precise, Enterprise made the rich blue dishes with white festoons that we previously attributed to a foreign source.

Columbian prided themselves on special designs like their Onyx White Enamel Ware, which was designed and produced especially to meet the requirements of the very popular white kitchen."

Of special interest to collectors are the brown Onyx biscuit trays and cutters. The trays have indentations for one dozen biscuits, which was claimed to:

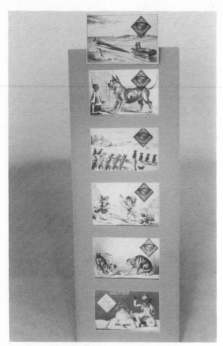

"Patent Granite Iron Ware" trade cards. Black and white. $8 each

Back cover of 1890s "Agate Iron Ware Cookbook." Note child's shopping bag with L & G Logo. $35

Look more tasty, bake better and best reflect the skill of the housewife when evenly cut and uniform in size. The "Onyx" Biscuit Cutter insures easier and quicker biscuit making, cuts the dough to fit spaces in the tray. The tray separates the biscuits so that the heat reaches all sides; they rise evenly and brown uniformly. This is only one of the many "Onyx" Enamel Utensils especially designed by Domestic Science Authorities.

Polar promised, "Color in the kitchen puts a smile in the work." Their ad in the April 1928 *Good Housekeeping* stated:

> Every woman of taste is delighted with the cheerfulness that gay colors impart to the kitchen — a hitherto rather uninteresting room. Brilliant hues found their way into the breakfast nook, and now they invade the kitchen in cooking utensils.

In the *Ladies' Home Journal*, May, 1925, NESCO offered a book to help plan, refurnish, or redecorate kitchens. *Nesco Better Kitchens* cost twenty-five cents.

Women were encouraged to relax and to take life easier. The Lisk roaster was the answer — one could rock and roast! A 1905 *Munsen's Magazine* ad portrayed a woman sitting in a rocker reading a book while the turkey roasted. The caption: "A roast means a rest to the owner of a Lisk roaster. Put the roast in the oven, look at the clock and rest."

Other ads claimed that their ware was easier to clean. No polishing, scouring, or hard rubbing was necessary; only hot water. Enamelware practically dried itself and always retained its clean, beautiful luster.

A full-page ad in *Good Housekeeping*, July 1914, illustrates how advertising appealed to women's concern for their families' prosperity. The long, detailed ad stated in part:

> There's such a thing as paying too much for your kitchen utensils — and very much such a thing as paying too little, if really intelligent economy is to rule your buying. How much did it cost — How long did it last, therefore, How much did it cost me per day — What work did it save — What cooking results did it give? These are questions the real kitchen economist must ask.
>
> The price of "Royal Granite Enameled Ware" is less than some because over twenty five years of experience, a really enormous production, and our secret inimitable process, make it possible, through manufacturing economics, for us to sell it at a fair price. It is more than some, because to cheapen the price, we would have to lower the quality, the durability, and therefore, the ultimate economy of the purchaser.

There was more, but you get the picture. A Lisk ad in 1905 stated:

> Actual tests show that a ten-pound piece of roast beef will weigh only eight pounds, or less, when roasted in the ordinary pan — a clear loss of two pounds, or one-fifth of the weight; at this rate you do not need to have roasts very often before this waste amounts to three or four dollars a month!

Republic said that their "Speedyheet" saved on fuel because this ware covered the burner completely, utilizing the heat that ordinarily escaped.

Advertisers offered homemakers samples, premiums, and trade incentives. "Granite Iron Ware" cookbooks were sent on request, according to the only magazine ad we know of by the St. Louis Stamping Company. This ad was in the June 9, 1892, *Youth Companion Magazine*. Cookbooks and books, such as *Kitchen Wisdom*, were frequently given.

A premium offer appeared in the September, 1880, issue of the *American Agriculturist*. Anyone selling six magazine subscriptions would receive a Manning, Bowman & Company butter dish. Eight subscriptions earned a water pitcher. And nineteen sales were worth an entire Granite Tea Set.

Merchants sold Maxwell's Peerless Kitchen Sets for ninety-nine cents with the purchase of five dollars worth of merchandise. There were coupons in flour sacks that could be redeemed for kitchen sets. And customers who purchased one dollar's worth of Granite Iron Ware could have a "Granie-ta" souvenir tray, dated 1884.

In 1910, the National Enameling and Stamping Company began publishing the *Nesco News*, which they claimed contained information dealers could turn into dollars. This magazine featured articles on selling techniques, samples of display cards, window trims, homespun philosophy, and classified ads.

In the January 1923 issue, there are articles on steel production and a sample page advertising *"Nesco Royal Granite Enameled Ware,"* again claiming that "The enamel mixture, too, is our own, containing real granite that helps to make the beautiful color, the smooth, non-porous surface, and the enduring quality."

Even though there was a large variety of advertising, the three companies that we followed closely had definite preferences. Lalance and Grosjean chose full-page magazine ads. The St. Louis Stamping Company preferred more permanent reminders of their products. By comparison with the other two companies, Vollrath did little advertising.

As we said in *Collectors' Showcase*, November/December 1983, advertising is invaluable. It provides us with evidence to clear up mysteries and settle controversies. And the pictures and captions help document pieces.

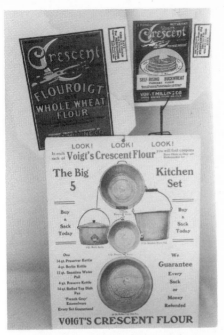

Flour sacks with coupons good for purchasing enamelware sets. **$3 each**
Store card. **$20**

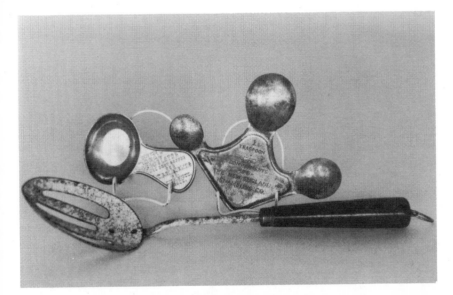

Gray slotted mixing spoon. **$35**
Coffee measure, "Use The 'IDEAL' PERCOLATOR For Best Coffee, The N.E. ENAMELING CO. Middletown, Conn." **$25**
Three-spoon measure, "1 Teaspoon, Compliments of The New England Enameling Co. ½, ¼." **$35**

Measuring cup, tin, embossed "National Enameling & Stamping Co." Graduated marking quarters and thirds. Soldered, tapered strap handle and pieced bottom. **$25**

Blue Lisk salesman's sample roaster with rack. **$195**
Lisk pinback dated 1898. **$25**

Catalog page is significant in that the trademark reads "Registered June 9th, 1874." This is the earliest mark we know of for manufacturing granite ware. **$35**

Early cookbook with display of "Granite Iron Ware" with metal trim. **$35**

"IRON-CLAD" postcard. **$15**
"IRON-CLAD" full-page ad. **$20**

Five French-type "Patent Granite Iron Ware" trade cards. Picture postcard of Lalance & Grosjean Manufacturing Company. **$15 each**

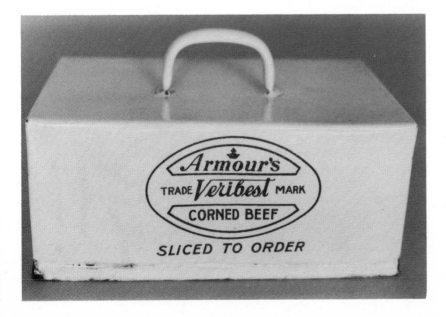

A Large Assortment of
ENAMEL WARE
DURABLE & CHEAP

Toy frying pan. **$15**

Folding chair. **$175**

Brown and cream Hershey dispenser.
$95

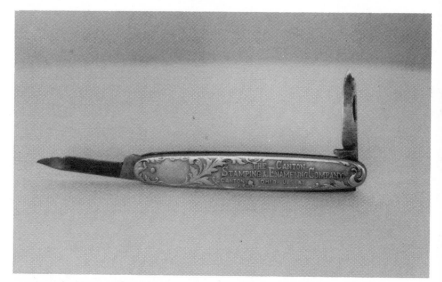

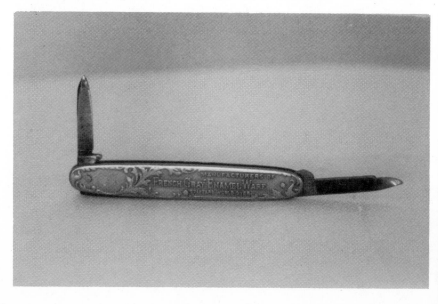

Pocket knife, "The Canton Stamping &
Enameling Company, Canton, Ohio
U.S.A." Other side: "Manufacturers of
French Gray Enamel Ware. Standard
World Over." **$50**

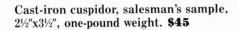

Buttermilk dispenser, cream and black with poppy, California's state flower. **$1,200**

"Nesco" flour sifter. **$10**
Tin match safe embossed "Nesco." **$45**

Enameled cast-iron teakettle, "Granite Iron Ware Pat May 30 76 and May 8 77." This 22″ tall teakettle hung over granite ware displays in stores. **$2,500 to $3,000**

Gray Quaker Oats cooker. Rare. **$200**

Tin toy or pin tray. **$15**

Other side: "Made by The REPUBLIC METALWARE Co. Formerly Sidney Shepard & Co. Founded 1836."

Top: "The Central Stamping Company" postcard sent to store owners advising that their salesman would pick up orders on October 19, 1909. **$15**
Bottom: Aluminum coated calling card with Iron Clad Manufacturing Company pictured. Other side mentions Nellie Bly, owner, and the "World's First Lady Industrialist." **$25**

"Calumet Baking Powder" Table, 15"x21"x17". **$200**

"IDEAL" embossed ashtray. **$35**

Tin bucket, "Patent Granite Iron Ware" and "Charter Oak Stoves," one gill size. Note soldered seam, pieced bottom, and wire bail. This lard-filled bucket was given away in the 1870s. **$50**

Tin bucket, opposite side.

Gray iron paperweight embossed "Your Warm Friend," compliments of Thatcher Manufacturing Company, makers of boilers, ranges and furnaces. **$85**

Ashtray, "The Moore Enameling and Manufacturing Co. West Lafayette, Ohio," gray and white. **$25**

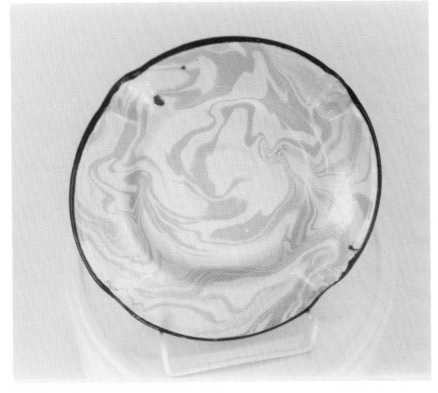

Bread was stored in airtight and mouse-proof containers long before waxed-paper-wrapped bakery bread (or light bread, as Southeners called it) was available. **$45**

Bread box, vented. **$45**

Bread raiser, blue and white with vented tin lid. **$125**

Bread box with hinged lid and brass handle. *Frisches Brot* (fresh bread), Germany. **$55**

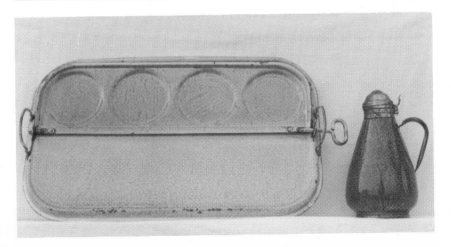

Pancake griddle, early L & G, hinged. **$175**
Syrup pitcher with tin cover and pouring spout, L & G. (Lalance and Grosjean Manufacturing Company). **$125**

This blue "New Perfection Toaster" was especially designed for use on the New Perfection kerosene stove. This was previously identified as a comfit pan, which is similar in design. **$48**

Churn, gray enameled, nine-gallon capacity. Manufactured by "Dickman and Elliot, Wapokeneta, Ohio." **$400- $700**

Muffin cups. These were filled with batter and placed in a biscuit pan. **ea. $15-$25**

Turban cake pans. Old baker's set of 8″ pans, heavily enameled. **$90**

These three cupcake pans were riveted onto a thin disk that fit into a round cake pan. They were used to make cupcakes from leftover batter or for testing batter to see if more flour was needed. **$35**

Butter Dish, "L & G Mfg Co" in oval. Hollow knob is part of the cover. This was offered in the 1920 catalog. **$150** Covered steamer with collapsible legs and bail handle. **$38**

Muffin pan. Unusual in that it only has four cups. **$45**

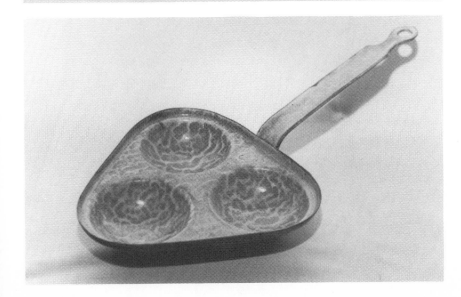

Egg fry pan. This is sometimes confused with an egg poacher. Egg poachers with individual removable cups were offered by Republic Stamping and Enameling Company, Canton, Ohio, in their 1904 catalog. They were covered pans with racks and cups. Metal egg poachers were sold by Sears, Roebuck and Company. They were similar in design; however, the egg poacher fit into the water pan and the handle on the egg poacher turned straight up and extended out over the side of the water pan. **$55**

Egg pan. **$55**
Portable stove with wick. The kerosene (coal oil) tank is made of enameled iron. **$165**

Boston milk kettle, L & G, also sold as a bar pitcher. **$110**

Fish tool, hollow handled with hook. **$25**
Turner, pierced with strap handle that has an eye and a hook. **$35**
Egg pan, four holes, with a support leg extending from handle. **$55**

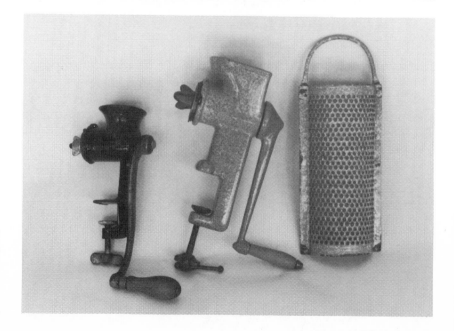

Black enameled "Nutter Butter Cutter." This is similar to a meat grinder, but it has fine blades for making peanut butter. **$38**
Bright green enameled food grinder. **$42**
Grater, gray with wire handle. **$55**

Snipe lipped L & G Agate Ware ladle. Rare. **$45**

Dippers. 9″ turned wooden handle was nailed into enameled ferrule which was riveted to cup. 13½″ handle was nailed into seamed enameled ferrule, which was riveted to cup. 9½″ turned wooden handle was nailed to a heavy enameled iron ferrule that was riveted to cup. **$60 to $100**

Skimmer, 14″. **$50**
Turner for eggs or cakes, 12″. **$200**
Strainer ladle, 13″. **$50**

Dipper, windsor, hollow handle. **$25**
Dipper used on farms and in breweries is extra strong, with heavy wood handle. **$48**
Ladle, with side for scraping. **$35**

Flaring dipper with hollow handle. **$25**
Farm or suds dipper. **$55**
L & G soup ladle with eyelet. **$28**

Spoons. Three in foreground are Mexican made and still available. **$1 to $2 each**
Pierced spoon, about twenty-five years old. **$8**
Mixing spoon, threaded handle with eyelet. **$18**
Mixing spoon with eyelet. **$15**
Mixing spoon, bright blue. **$6**

114

Soup ladle with metal rim and extended ferrule that was fitted with a turned wooden handle. **$100**

Top: Grocer's scoop. **$65**
Granite iron ware scoop with flat bottom and bent strap handle. **$85**
Bottom: Agate thumb scoop. **$65**
L & G confectioner's scoop with metal ferrule and wooden handle. **$100**

Mixing spoon. This heavy old gray spoon was made with a riveted joint at the bowl and handle, the stress point, which made it a poor design. **$18**

Pie pan marked "Pat. June 7, 1892." Note spot where Mendet was applied. **$18**

Salt box. Shown in early L & G cookbook. Lid is missing. **$175**

Salt box with hinged lid and hollow knob. **$165**

Salt boxes, early Agate Iron Ware and Granite Iron Ware. They have applied strap handles and seamed bottoms and bodies. The heavy tin lids do not screw on but are so precisely made they are very secure. These boxes were also made for sifting flour over meat and sprinkling powdered sugar. They were sometimes called dredges. A pepper box, the same height and half the diameter of the salt box, was also made. Box is the term used in the early catalogs for what we now call shakers. **$175 each**

Measure, one quart, 4″x4¼″, stamped "For Household Use Only." Applied lip. **$28**

Measuring cups.
Bottom: Seamed Cups differ in the length of the handle threads.
Top: Note riveted, threaded strap handle. **$35 each**

Measuring cups.
Left: Note welded and riveted wire handle.
Right: Seamed cup, riveted strap handle, embossed letters.
Top: Tapered cup with small welded handle. **$35 each**

Measure ½ cup (one gill), "For Household Use Only." This measure is especially collectible. **$60**

Measuring cups, designed for measuring thirds.
Left: This Agate Ware cup has been coated with an opaque coat that obscures the original gray finish.
Right: Agate iron ware cup. Note application of handles. **$35 each**

Measure, "General Steel Wares Ltd 1 Pint."Canada. Copper rivet on handle marked "GR 7J9. Applied lip fits across front only. **$35**

Complete set of NESCO measures, one-eighth quart to one gallon. Collector spent fifteen years completing set. **$300**

Gray oil can. **$65**
Kitchen or shop scale with original gray enameled pan. **$95**

Tumbler, seamless agate shown in 1886 L & G catalog. **$38**
Ice cream measure, signed "Extra Agate L&G Mfg Co." Described in 1894 L & G Catalog as one pint and one quart ice cream measure, and also as a child's mug. **$45**

Gelatin molds. The 1894 L & G catalog advertised seven sizes, from 6¾"x5" to 10½"x8". At this time, cooks were preparing a gelatin dessert with powder, sugar and fruit juice. Note stand. **$38 to $75 each**

White mold for gelatin or mousse dessert. **$65**

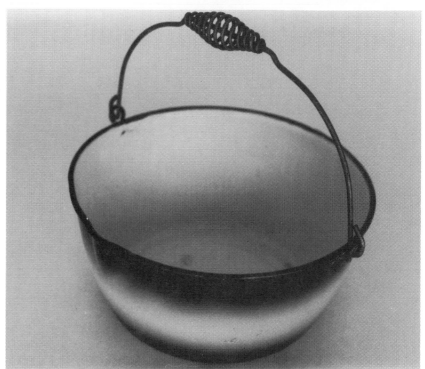

Preserve kettle, BlueBelle Ware with wire bail and Alaska handle. **$65**

Columbian roaster, 8″x15″x11″. Most companies marked their roaster lids — a great way to advertise. **$45**

Roaster with wire handles, domed lid, and unusual crown-shaped knob. **$35**

NESCO roaster with name embossed on either side of handle on lid. **$28**

Savory roaster with name embossed on handles as well as lid. **$35**

Wedge-shaped strainer with three iron feet. $48
Footed sink strainer. $35

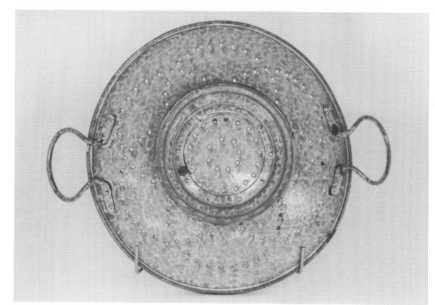

Colander, footed with riveted welded wire handle. Underside view. $45

Steamer insert. $18

Colander, three footed, gray with dark blue trim. **$15**

Strainer with pierced hang-tab and handle. Only bottom is pierced. **$35**

Basket of two-piece set used for deep frying. **$33**

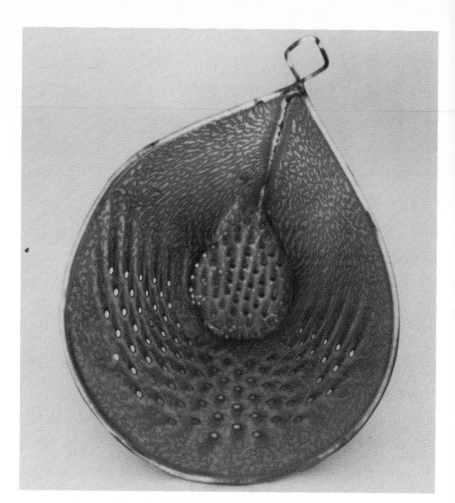

Sink strainer, teardrop shape. Wire hanger runs under entire rim for additional strength and to finish off the edge. **$45**

Double boiler steamer, cream and green. The excellent design and quality of this steamer enables it to be used as a strainer or colander. **$23**

Colander with applied fast feet. **$14**

Octagonal strainer, three legs, side handle, and attached drain pan. This unusual pan was particularly useful to the cook who had no sink. **$80**

Strainer pan or steamer insert. Used for draining cottage cheese or steaming vegetables. **$18**

Asparagus/corn boiler with rack, L & G Manufacturing Company. **$75**

Serving

Three-piece dinner bucket, mottled blue and white. **$150**
Muffin pan, eight cups, blue and white. **$200**

Agate dinner carrier. This was advertised in the 1886 L & G Catalog. There were two sizes. The smallest had three food sections, which were 7″ in diameter. The large one, pictured, had four 8″ diameter sections. The sections fit into a frame, which had a vented base that could be placed on a stove for heating. **$150**
Muffin pan with turk's head or turban cups. This unusual item may have been custom-made. **$200**

Silk screening. Tray is 19″x23½″. **$250**

Dinner bucket with gray enamel cover fitted with a tin cup lid. "Republic Metalware" paper label. **$65**

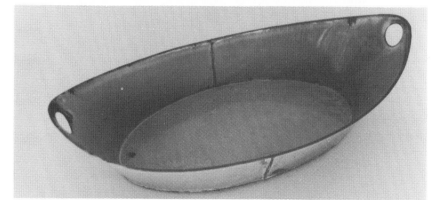

Agate bread tray shown in *L & G Illustrated Price Guide*, August, 1886. Note side seams and pieced bottom. **$65**

Stenciling on rare advertising tray. **$350**

Gravy boat, L & G. Also made in white with blue trim. Desirable and difficult to find. **$125**

Sugar bowl, gray with black enameled knob and thin strap handles applied by rivets. **$85**

Biscuit cutter, 2½″, blue and white.
Heirloom
Sugar bowl, blue and white with dark bead. **$95**

Sugar canister. Holland. Texture matches a Dutch wall rack in Book One. **$35**

Set of NESCO covered ice box dishes. These were advertised for 15¢ each in the 1920s. **$35 each**

Bowl. Height, 5″; diameter, 8″. **$80**
Tea caddy with slip-on tin lid. **$55**

Coffee canister with slip-on tin lid. Near-mint condition. **$95**

Beer tray with drip grooves. This was later advertised as a tray, with no mention of beer. **$100**

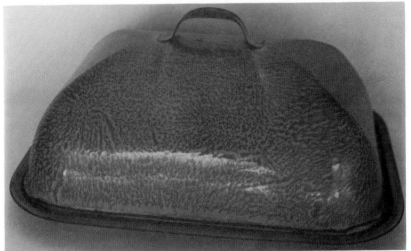

L & G covered platter with seamless lid. Height, 8″; width, 14″; length, 20″. This was also available in white with a blue border and brown with a white lining, and was sold as Turquoise Pearl-Agate, El-an-ge and Agate. **$250**

Soup tureen with wooden handles, stamped "ACME" and marked with decal "Granite Iron Ware Pat Oct 9, '94 and July 21, '96." Six rivets hold foot to bowl. Lid is not slotted. *L & G Illustrated Catalog*, August, 1886, offered this same tureen. **$175**

Soup tureen, bright blue with white lining and black bead. **$175**

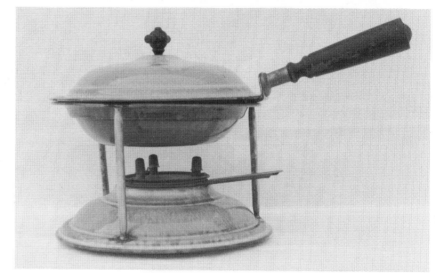

Chafing dish. This straight-leg model was shown in the *Agate Cook Book*, 1890, as part of "The Sawtelle Agate Chafing Dish Outfit," which consisted of the "chafing dish, an oval tray, soup bowl, strainer, soup plate and a measuring cup packed in a neat wooden box for $5.00 per set." **$225**

Granite Iron Ware Improved Chafing Dish. Asbestos burner is missing. The St. Louis Stamping Company and Lalance and Grosjean made these in their early period. **$200**

Bellboy or hotel pitcher. Wire bail, wood grip handle and a wire tipping handle. Each ear was made of two pieces of metal riveted onto pitcher. **$75**

Kerosene stove with early goose-necked teapot and one wick. **$300**

Teakettle, cast iron with footed round bottom. This is the oldest piece in Welch collection. It has an original porcelain knob on the sliding lid. The lid is imprinted "Sidney Hollow Ware Co." The spiral wire on the bail, later called "The Alaska," was designed to withstand the range-top heat and fire from the open hearth or campfire. Rare. **$125**

Decals on coffeepot. **$38**

Square teakettle. This unusual teakettle was bought at a London flea market. It had just come out of an estate and still had water in it. **$200**

Teakettle with locking device to hold wooden bail handle away from the heat. Whitehead said that this type was made by reversing a preserve kettle, turning up the edge to fit the bottom, cutting holes for the lid and spout, and finally attaching the ears. **$45**

Teakettle. The advent of the kerosene-fueled kitchen stove brought about the need for a flat-bottomed "hugger" teakettle that would keep the flame from spreading up around the kettle and, at the same time, not smother the flame. This kettle was designed to fill this need. It was offered in the 1910 NESCO catalog in gray, but not in their Blue Ribbon three-coated line. **$75**

"Elite, Austria" teapot, has many jewel-like colors. Principally dark brown, highlighted by veining of blue, green, yellow, white. **$75**

"Duchess" coffeepot by Vollrath. Pit bottom, early 1900s. Beautiful tortoise-like splotches of blue amid soft brown-and-white veining. **$95**

Demitasse and saucer. **$35**
Individual iron handled teapot. **$150**

Teapot and coffeepot with crown cover
wire knobs on tin domed lid. **$48 each**

"Mikasa Grande Chef" 2.5 quart kettle.
Ejiri, Japan, 1982, silver gray. **$50**

Manning-Bowman coffee biggin. Two perforated discs and a fine wire screen regulate the flow of hot water, thereby achieving the steeping, triple drip process. **$375**

Coffee mill with raised gray granite open hopper and hardwood box with dovetailed corners. The hopper has an L & G appearance. The 1894 catalog offers coffee mills, but not gray hoppers. **$250.**

"Tea Reservoir" stamped on bottom, also "Made in China" and sketch of a tea garden and Chinese characters. Cream colored and old. **$20**

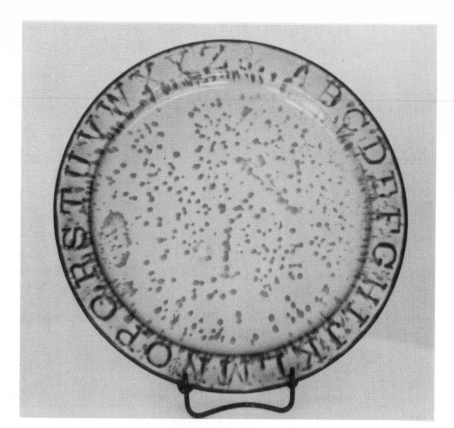

Embossed ABC plate found in a locked trunk sold at auction. When the trunk was opened, a number of these plates were found inside, wrapped in 1902 paper. Plates were advertised in L & G and St. Louis Stamping Company catalogs and cookbooks. **$400**

Baby plates with a considerable amount of flux. **$15 each**

Children's plates with decals. Campbell Soup Kids, signed "Grace Drayton." **$38 each**

Souvenir tumbler and plate with Indian decals. **$35 each**

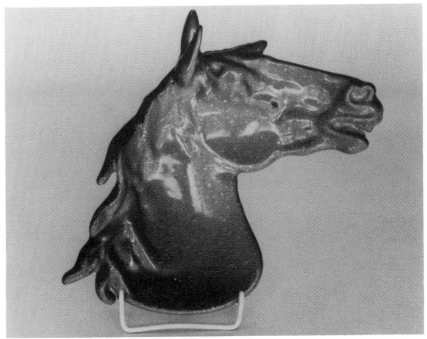

Heavy gray iron spoonrest. **$65**

Blue ironrest. **$45**
Gray ironrest. **$45**

Turtle iron trivet. **$65**
Cat spoonrest. **$55**
Gray iron incense burner. **$45**

Teapot shelf from Moffat Range, gray.
$35

Enameled iron trivet, gray. **$55**

Household Items

Fastfooted agate basin and pitcher offered in 1880s *Agate Cook Book*, L & G Manufacturing Company. **$95**

Water carrier in L & G catalog, 1886, sold as part of Prince and King toilet sets at $3 each. Used to carry hot water. Covered spout prevents heat loss and spilling. **$150**

Bathtub, 21″x27″x10″. **$75**

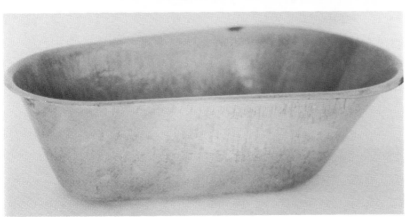

Bidet with nickel-plated drain and stopper. This fit into a folding frame. **$225**

Shaving tub with attached soap compart-
ment. **$65**

Shaving tub with brush and soap com-
partment. **$50**

Apple green toothbrush holder. **$25**
Tumbler, white with blue trim. **$10**

L & G bathroom fixture with nickel and
copper fittings. This was plumbed and
had overflow drain. L & G also made single, double, and triple laundry tubs with
corrugated fronts for scrubbing. **$175**

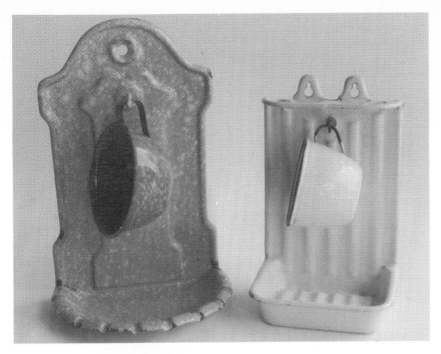

Gray comb case. L & G offered this in Japanned Tin in 1894, but we do not know when it was first enameled. **$165**

Gray wall rack with cup. **$45**
White rack and cup. Rack has slots for four toothbrushes. These racks are called "soap and flannel" in England, where a flannel square for washing hangs on the hook. **$38**

Beer tray. **$65**
Soap dish, "Extra Agate Nickel Steel Ware." **$75**

Iron-handled spit cup, featured in 1894 L & G catalog. **$75**
Gray spit cup. These were used by tobacco-chewing travelers and lady snuff dippers. **$60**

Soap dish, 4¾"x⅝". Pictured in L & G catalogs in 1886 and 1894 as Agate Iron Ware and in 1903 as Agate Steel Ware. **$65**

Gray irrigator or douche. **$75**

Combinet lid. 1886 L & G catalog features odor-free agate improved slop jar lid with valve. **$23**

Two-liter petrol container, light blue and white with gold lettering. France. Held oil for lamp or stove use. **$125**

Candlestick pictured in 1916 *Republic Stamping and Enameling Company Catalog.* **$75**
Candlestick pictured in 1894 L & G catalog. **$75**

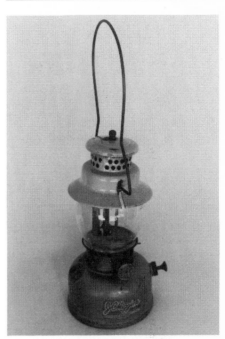

"J.C. Higgins" gasoline lantern, gray enameled shade. **$68**

Top: Utensil rack, holds potholders or stove cloths. Germany. **$55**
Bottom: Wall rack. **$55**

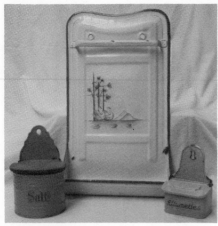

Blue salt box with wooden lid. **$110**
Utensil rack, white with blue trim. **$125**
Blue match box, gray trim. **$60**

Ash shovel. **$25**
Rack. **$55**
Fish turner. **$35**

Gray spoon and spice rack. **$65**

Wall rack with ladles and flesh fork (rare). **$175**

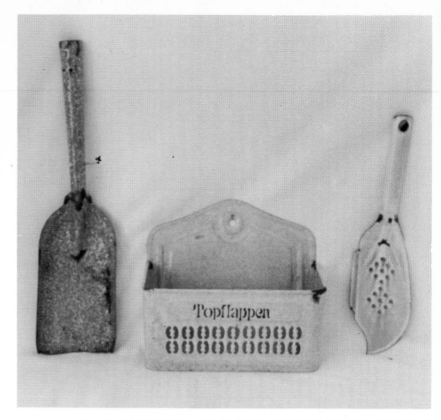

Lid racks with potholder hooks. **$125 each**

Towel rack for hands, china, cutlery and glasses. France. The use of several dishcloths was common in the American kitchens before running water was available. The black from wood and coal stoves stained dishcloths, so great-grandmother's insistence on using the right towel is understandable. **$75.**

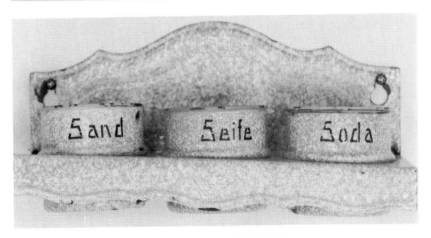

Wall rack for sand, soap and soda. German. **$65**

Beer glass stand, blue and white, L & G. **$95**
Blue-and-white mustard server. **$150**
Glue pot, L & G. **$250**
Mustard jar. **$150**

Bird feeder, 2″x2½″. **$25**

American military helmet. **$500**

Flasks, 5″ and 4″. **$125 each**

Manning-Bowman

Teapot with metal breast and lid-rest on handle. **$325**

Teapot. Etched, planished tin with gray bottom. **$325**

Statue of Liberty coffeepot pictured in 1885 catalog, commemorating October 28, 1886, dedication. **$295**

Belle teapot with white metal trim and copper base. **$325**

Blue coffee or tea server, wooden knob and handle. **$175**

Biggin with white metal trim. Belle-shaped gray bottom is identical to teapot with scalloped collar. **$375**

Goblet, one of two that were sold as a set with double ice pitcher, tray, and a waste bowl. **$100**
Melon-shaped sugar bowl. Lid missing. **$175**

Spooner, sugar and creamer, white with nickel-plated white metal mountings. **$75 each**

Caster set, unusually large and mint condition. **$900**

Cuspidor pictured in 1885 catalog. **$200**

Metal trimmed tray with porcelain handles. **$400**
Metal trimmed mug. **$125**

Caster set, "Patent Perfection Granite Iron Ware." Dinner casters were recommended as more durable and not affected by acids of vinegar or mustard. They were made in four styles with four or five bottles. Larger decorated pearl agateware dinner casters were available in two designs, plain or fancy handles, and five or six bottles. Pictured in 1885 catalog. **$750**

Bibliography

Benham and Stoutenborough 1895 Catalog. New York: Reproduced by Antique and Hobby Book Publications, Amador City, Calif.

Beuttenmuller, Doris Rose Henle. "The Granite City Steel Company: History of an American Enterprise." Ph.D. diss., St. Louis University. St. Louis: Eden, 1954.

Breakfast, Luncheon and Dinner Cook Book. Milwaukee, Wisc.: Advertising Department, National Enameling and Stamping Company, 1915.

Bryant, E. E. "Set and Grinding of Porcelain Enamel." *The Enamelist* 27-1 (Spring, 1950): 18-25.

Butler Brothers Wholesale Catalogs. New York: Butler Brothers, December 1905, Number 551; August 1907, Number 622; October 1908, Number 684; Mid-Summer 1912, Number 1010; Mid-Summer 1913, Number 1116; July, 1915, Number 1323; January 1917, Number 1460.

Central Stamping Company Catalog #47. New York.

Bates, William S. "Pennsylvania Ceramics Date Back to 1683." *Ceramic Industry Magazine* (May, 1975).

Clawson, C. D. "Notes and Comment." *The Enamelist* 26-3 (Summer, 1949):2.

Compton's Encyclopedia, 1971 ed., s.v. "enameling" and "iron."

Connare, Harold P. "Cost Reduction in Porcelain Enamel Operations Through Product and Process Control." *The Enamelist* 27-2-3 (Summer-Fall, 1950):20-27.

Cream City Ware Champion. Milwaukee: Geuder, Paeschke and Frey Company, February, 1911.

DeVoe, Shirley Spaulding. *The Art of The Tinsmith*. Exton, Pennsylvania: Schiffer Publishing Limited, 1981.

Dictionary of American Biography, s.v. "Niedringhaus, Frederick Gottlieb."

Duncan, R. F. "Colors In Porcelain Enamel." *The Enamelist* 26-3 (Summer, 1949):17-19.

Favorite Stoves and Ranges Company, 1914 General Catalog. Piqua, Ohio.

Federal Enameling and Stamping Company Catalog, 1924. Pittsburgh, Pennsylvania.

Grand Union Tea Company Sales Brochure. Brooklyn Borough, New York.

"A History, A Mission, A Future." Granite City Steel, Granite City, Illinois 62040.

Granite Iron Ware Cook Book. St. Louis, Missouri: St. Louis Stamping Company, 1885.

Alexandersson, Gunnar. *Geography of Manufacturing*. Englewood Cliffs, N.J. Prentice-Hall Inc., 1967.

Harrison, Molly. *The Kitchen in History*. New York. Charles Scribner and Sons, 1972.

Herrick, Christine Terhune. *Kitchen Experiences*. New York. National Enameling and Stamping Company, 1903.

"Dolly's Favorite, Cast Range, A Complete Range for Little Girls, The Favorite Stove and Range Co., Piqua, Ohio," featured in 1915 catalog.

Howe, E. E. and Glen H. McIntyre. "Glossary, Enamel Division." The American Ceramic Society. Mimeo.

Ingram-Richardson Manufacturing Company, 1939 Catalog of Table Tops. New York, New York.

Iron Clad Manufacturing Company Catalog. New York: 1897.

Ketcham, Howard. "Kitchens Set a Color Trap." *The Enamelist* 27-1 (Spring, 1950): 10-13.

Lalance and Grosjean Manufacturing Company Price Catalog. New York: Macgowan and Slipper, August 1886.

Lalance and Grosjean Manufacturing Company Agate Cook Book. New York: Macgowan and Slipper, January 1, 1890.

Lalance and Grosjean Manufacturing Company Catalog. New York: Macgowan and Slipper, 1894.

Lalance and Grosjean Manufacturing Company Price Catalog. 1903.

Lalance and Grosjean Manufacturing Company Catalog. New York: Bartlett Orr Press, 1922.

Lifshey, Earl. *The Housewares Story.* Chicago: National Housewares Manufacturers Association, 1973.

Lisk Manufacturing Company, Limited, Catalogue No. 60. Canandaigua, New York, August 1931.

Marshall Field and Company 1914 Doll Catalog. Cumberland, Maryland 21502: Hobby House Press, 1980.

McIntyre, G. H. "Porcelain Enamel As a Corrosion Resistant Coating For Metals." *The Enamelist* 27-2-3 (Summer-Fall, 1950):3-9.

McLaren, H. D. "Porcelain Enamel As A Protective Finish." *The Enamelist* 26-3 (Summer, 1949):8-13.

McLuhan, Marshall. *Understanding Media: The Extensions of Man.* New York, London, Sydney, Toronto: McGraw-Hill Book Company, 1964.

Montgomery Ward and Company Mid-Winter Sale Catalog. Oakland, Calif., 1927.

The National Cyclopaedia of American Biography, s.v. "Grosjean, Florian," "Niedringhaus, Albert William," and "Niedringhaus, Frederick G."

National Enameling and Stamping Company Catalog. New York, 1910.

New Perfection Cook-Book. The Cleveland Foundry Company, 1912.

Norvell Shapleigh Company Wholesale Catalog. St. Louis, Missouri.

Oxford Universal Dictionary, 3rd ed., s.v. "g. ware."

Parr, Leslie, Andrea Hicks, and Marie Stareck. *Best of Sears Collectibles 1905-1910.* New York: Arno Press, 1976.

Reed, Ann, International Trade Commission, Chemical Division, Washington, D.C., telephone conversation with author, 23 August, 1985.

Republic Metalware Company Catalog. New York, 1910.

Republic Stamping and Enameling Company. Revised Schedule of Prices for 1916. Canton, Ohio.

Rittenhouse, Mignon. *The Amazing Nellie Bly.* Freeport, N.Y.: Books For Libraries Press, 1956.

Savory Prize Recipe Book. The Republic Metalware Company, 1918. Buffalo, N.Y.

Schreiber, Karl. "Porcelain Enamel And Organic Finishes." *The Enamelist* 26-3 (Summer 1949): 22-24.

Sears Roebuck and Company Fall 1900 Catalog, Number 110. Chicago, Illinois: Reproduced by DBI Books, Inc., Northfield, Ill., 1976.

Sears Roebuck and Company 1908 Catalog Number 117, The Great Price Maker. Edited by Joseph J. Schroeder, Jr. Chicago, Illinois: The Gun Digest Company, 1969.

Sirovy, George and Edmund P. Czolgos. "Mottled Enameled Finishes Obtained by Precipitation of Various Color-producing Salts." *The American Ceramic Society*, vol 28, no. 6 (June 15, 1949).

Ukers, William H. *All About Coffee*, Second Edition. New York: The Tea and Coffee Trade Journal Company. Burr Printing House, 1935.

U.S. Department of Commerce, Patent and Trademark Office, Washington, D.C. Holley, George W., of Niagara, New York. March 10, 1857; Burrough, George A., Providence, Rhode Island, May 30, 1871; Vollrath, Carl A. W., Sheboygan, Wisconsin, November 19, 1889; Vollrath, Jacob J., Sheboygan, Wisconsin, December 6, 1881; Niedringhaus, Frederick G. and Niedringhaus, William F., St. Louis, Missouri, May 30, 1876, April 17, 1877, January 23, 1877, January 23, 1877, May 1, 1877, April 10, 1877, July 3, 1877; Niedringhaus, William F., St. Louis, Missouri, July 31, 1877; Milligan, John C., South Orange, N.J., Assignor to Lalance and Grosjean Manufacturing Company, New York, June 16, 1874; and Manning, Edward B., Meriden, Connecticut, December 24, 1895.

Vitrearc Catalogue Number 978, Enamels For The Artist, Newport, Kentucky, 41072: Ceramic Coating Company, 1978.

Vogelzang, Vernagene and Evelyn Welch. "The Daily Reflections of Graniteware Advertising." *Collectors' Showcase*, vol. 3, no. 2 (November/December 1983).

Jacob J. Vollrath Manufacturing Company Catalog. Sheboygan, Wisc., 1904.

About the Authors

At left: Evelyn Welch, granite ware collector, expert, and pricer. *Right:* Vernagene Vogelzang, freelance writer and photographer.